GW00994032

AGER'S WAY
TO EASY ELEGANCE

BY
STANLEY AGER
AND
FIONA ST. AUBYN

Produced by James Wagenvoord

Published by The Bobbs-Merrill Company, Inc.
Indianapolis   New York

Copyright © 1980 by James Wagenvoord Studio, Inc.,
10 East 49th Street, New York, N.Y. 10017.
All rights reserved, which includes the right to reproduce
this book or portions thereof in any form whatsover.

Produced by James Wagenvoord Studio, Inc.
Editor-in-chief: James Wagenvoord
Design: Marta Norman
Senior editor: Dinah Stevenson
Assistant editor: Anne Dodd
Illustrations: Stephen Laughlin, James R. Jones
Art assistants: Jerry Harding, Lisa Albert, Rita-Sue Bell

Published by The Bobbs-Merrill Company, Inc.
Indianapolis   New York

Manufactured in the United States of America
First printing

Library of Congress Cataloging in Publication Data

Ager, Stanley.
Ager's Way to easy elegance.

1. Home economics—Handbooks, manuals, etc.
I. St. Aubyn, Fiona, joint author.   II. Title.
III. Title: Way to easy elegance.

TX159.A35   640   80-673

ISBN 0-672-52665-4

For Barbara, Mary and Piers, with thanks.

NOTES

Throughout the book references to the second lord are to the second Lord St. Levan, and references to the third lord are to the third Lord St. Levan. The fourth Lord St. Levan presently lives at St. Michael's Mount, and we thank him for all his assistance in the making of this book.

In general, references to Her Ladyship are to the Dowager Lady St. Levan, the wife of the third lord. We thank her for her generous support and encouragement.

We are extremely grateful to the many people who gave us their time and insight.

Very special thanks must go to both the St. Aubyn and Ager families, whose help and understanding have proved invaluable. We are particularly grateful to James St. Aubyn and the Hon. Hilaria St. Aubyn. We would also like to express our gratitude to Mme. Armand Gazel, Miss Iva Dundas and the Balmer family of Marazion.

Special thanks must also go to Major John Baxendale, JoAnne G. Blackwelder, Helen Greene, Mrs. Hill, Linda Hodgson, Marley Hodgson, Carolyn Price Horton, Jean Koefoed, Mrs. Murphy, Norman Rothman, Frank Yardley.

Lastly, we express our appreciation to the following firms and organizations for their cooperation during the creation of this book: Cartier, Inc., New York, for the table setting shown on page 111. The British Museum; Alfred Dunhill of London, Inc.; Hammacher Schlemmer; Harrods Ltd.; S.C. Johnson and Son, Inc.; the Library of Congress; James Lock and Co., Ltd.; Henry Poole and Co.; Procter and Gamble; Nat Sherman, Tobacconist; Trafalgar Ltd.; A. and H. Page, Jewelers.

CONTENTS

AGER'S WAY

In 1975 I retired, after fifty-three years in service. Barbara and I moved out of our house on St. Michael's Mount, where we had lived for thirty years, and into one in Marazion, the village opposite the castle. We left the Mount on a Friday and had a house-warming party on the Sunday. It had taken us exactly two days to establish ourselves so completely that we didn't have to look for anything. Our friends were amazed. "It feels as though you've been here all your life!" they said. But it was simply a question of experience; we were used to moving house from having been in service. At the start of the London season, the staff were sent up in the afternoon to have the house ready for the family in the evening. We'd arrive to find the house in dust sheets, but by the time the family arrived for dinner, you would never know that anyone had been away.

At first I didn't feel right being out of uniform and in casual clothes in the morning; otherwise, I was content to retire. After all, I have traveled the world, lived in some magnificent houses and been lucky with my employers. But I still miss the staff. They fought amongst themselves and always caused me far more trouble than the Lord and Lady—yet I miss them most of all.

I was fourteen when I entered service in 1922. I began as hall-boy—the lowest servant of all—in Lord Coventry's household at Croome Court. On my first day it seemed like a house full of servants; there were some forty people of all ages working there. Everyone was friendly except the housekeeper—she didn't want anything to do with new boys. But she treated her youngest girls just the same way I was treated by the butler, and most butlers were courteous people.

I chose to work for Lord Coventry because he raced in partner-ship with his daughter, Lady Barbara Smith, and I have always been interested in horse racing. I come from Newmarket, a town north of London that is the home of British horse racing. My father was a head stableman and my brother an apprentice jockey. At one time I thought more about going into racing than about going into service, but after my parents died, entering service seemed the best way of supporting myself.

At the beginning I did most of my work in the servants' quarters at the back of the house. I didn't go to the front where the family lived, except for the dining room, until I had worked at Croome Court for six months. When I did, the flowers in the reception rooms struck me first of all. I can still remember the smell of the carnations. I had never seen carnations in such quantity before, and they were all colors—even yellow, and I haven't seen many yellow ones since. I was awed by the general opulence—the silver candlesticks and inkstands on the writing desks, the tapestries on the walls and the thick rugs, which were quite different from the stone tiles I was used to walking on.

It was not until I worked at the front of the house that I saw the family to speak to. The only time I saw them before that was at prayers, which were held in the dining room at nine o'clock after we laid the table for breakfast. At the end the lady of the house always said, "God make my servants dutiful." Then the family left the room and we rushed like mad to get breakfast on the table.

At fourteen, I wasn't considered young to start work. A lad was usually hallboy until he was fifteen and a half, then he became steward's room boy or third footman. The hallboy and steward's room boy learnt their trade by waiting on members of staff, and the hallboy looked after the butler's clothes. Only the grander houses had a steward's room boy, and few of them had as many as forty servants. Most houses had between twelve and fifteen staff members.

How quickly a lad was promoted depended on his ability rather than on his age. Most third and second footmen were very young footmen. Their duties included serving at table, cleaning silver and caring for clothes. The first footman was usually in his mid-twenties and acted as an assistant to the butler. Very few footmen became butlers until they were in their thirties. Before that a footman might valet the gentleman of the house. Then when he became butler, his most important duty was to see that the house ran smoothly.

Most young servants moved to a different house after about a year or so to gain promotion and to experience how various houses were run. A servant who was looking for another job became very snobbish about the family; we wanted someone who had several houses so we could travel round the country. Two houses weren't really enough. And they had to go to London in the London season–if they didn't have a house in London, we wouldn't look at that job either. We wanted London because of the lovely parties and because in town we could get out more and spend all the money we had saved in the country. This wasn't very much, as salaries were small–from fifteen to twenty pounds a year, which the hallboy received, to a butler's ninety pounds a year.

I left Lord Coventry to work for Lady Barbara Smith as steward's room boy. I stayed there a year before becoming third footman to the Pikes. The first guest I looked after for the Pikes was television pioneer John Logie Baird. He arrived with two scruffy suitcases and preferred a cheap brand of cigarettes to some excellent cigars after dinner. I didn't think my tip would amount to much. But when he left, he gave me five pounds–more than double my month's wages.

Next I was second footman to Sir Bryan Godfrey-Faussett, who was at one time equerry to King George V. Then in 1926 I went to

Lord Dunsany, a well-known author and playwright. He lived at Dunsany Castle, County Meath, Ireland, and his country house in England was Dunstall Priory in Kent. I began as second footman and valet to his eldest son. After a couple of years, when I was only nineteen, I was promoted to first footman and valet to Lord Dunsany.

I remember a time when H. G. Wells came to stay and the table-cloth accidentally caught fire. H. G. Wells was up in an instant and out of the window. The butler appeared and simply put the fire out with a damp cloth. I don't know whether this had anything to do with it, but I never saw H. G. Wells at Dunsany again.

I was at Dunsany for four years in all before leaving in 1930 to become full-time valet to the second Lord St. Levan. He lived in St. Michael's Mount, a castle just off the southern coast of England, in Cornwall. The Mount is about a quarter of a mile from the mainland. It can be reached by causeway eight hours out of twenty-four, but at high tide the sea is fifteen feet deep in the center of the causeway and the Mount becomes an island.

I took the job because I had never been to Cornwall and the second lord said he traveled. I went all round the world with him. Wherever he wanted to go, he just went. If it was cold when we returned to England, we'd pop off again. I made all the arrangements, bought the tickets and more or less made the world smooth for him and his party.

A valet was almost always a bachelor because so much of his time was spent traveling with his employer. So in 1933 after I married Barbara, who was parlormaid at the castle, I left the Mount for my first butlering job. I was twenty-six. For two years I worked for Mr. Dunkels, who was head of the Diamond Corporation, and Barbara worked as head parlormaid (the female equivalent of a butler) in another household.

I left in 1935 to become butler to Colonel Trotter, who lived at Charterhall, Berwickshire, Scotland. The house was a halfway stop for Princess Alice, who frequently stayed with us on her way to visit the Queen at Balmoral. Barbara and I were given a cottage on the estate. Our two daughters, Jill and Brenda, were born there, and we lived there for twelve years. During that time the war came, and I went into the army.

Soon after I returned at the end of the war, Colonel Trotter died. While I was mulling over my future, I received a letter from the third Lord St. Levan, who had succeeded his uncle at the Mount. He wrote asking me to come back as his butler. I said I'd come back for three months, which turned into nearly thirty years!

In my day we knew exactly what we had to do and what our roles were. The person who presided over the entire house was the lady of the house. Her three principals were the butler, the house-keeper and the cook: if there were arrangements to be discussed, she would see us in that order. The butler oversaw the pantry staff (the footmen, steward's room boy and hallboy), the housekeeper oversaw the housemaids and the stillroom maids (the women who made the preserves and cakes–a room was set aside for this) and the cook or chef oversaw the kitchen and the kitchen maids.

The housekeeper looked after the household linen. She was responsible for the staff quarters, whereas the butler was in charge of the front of the house. Normally butler, housekeeper and cook worked closely together, but if any of the three disliked each other, there was trouble. And some housekeepers could be quite nasty. They were lonely people and nearly always spinsters, al-though they were always called "Mrs." as a mark of respect. Cooks were also addressed in this manner. A cook was usually very bad-tempered; if she wasn't struggling against a clock, she was struggling against an oven. A cook seldom stayed at a house as long as the housekeeper, and if she did she was likely to be rather a tyrant. Nine times out of ten a butler or housekeeper stayed at the same house for years–perhaps thirty or forty years.

Next in line to the butler and housekeeper were the valet and lady's maid. Up until the second war any gentleman of any

consequence had a valet, and every lady had a lady's maid. The sons were looked after by the footmen and the daughters by the younger lady's maid, who was also the head housemaid. Footmen also looked after gentlemen guests who traveled without their valet, and housemaids looked after visiting ladies who traveled without their maid.

The head housemaid was directly beneath the lady's maid in rank, and she was equal to the first footman. The second housemaid was equal to the second footman and the third housemaid equal to the third footman. There might be seven housemaids in all, and the younger housemaids were equal to the steward's room boy and the hallboy. On the kitchen side of the house, the first kitchen maid was directly beneath the cook and equal to the first footman; the second and third kitchen maid were equal to the second and third footman. The scullery maid, who prepared the vegetables for cooking and washed the pots and the pans, was on a par with the hallboy.

As a rule, the large houses had footmen and a butler to oversee them, and the smaller houses had parlormaids and a head parlormaid. Parlormaids and footmen were never mixed, as they did the same work–the second parlormaid ranked with the first footman and the third parlormaid with the second footman. Most head parlormaids only had two parlormaids under them. The drawback to parlormaids was that they weren't able to do the same heavy work as footmen. A man would have to come in daily to carry coal or lift heavy leaves from the dining room table.

Our uniforms were provided by the family. A hallboy wore a dark gray flecked suit, which we called a salt and pepper but was officially described as a morning suit. Every male member of staff had one of these in his cupboard.

In addition to his salt and pepper the steward's room boy had a dark blue coat similar to a bellhop's jacket, which he wore with black box-cloth trousers. A footman wore a salt and pepper when he was working at the back of the house, for instance cleaning silver. Whenever he was waiting on the family he wore livery. A valet usually only wore a salt and pepper. Until the mid-1920s a butler wore a gray morning tailcoat with a cutaway front over a pair of gray striped trousers. After that time, a butler would wear a black evening tailcoat all day long. In the evening he changed from the gray trousers into a pair of black trousers with a fine silk line running down the side.

When I was a footman, the senior staff stood very much on their dignity, and the rest of the staff were acutely aware of their status within the house. No one could help out anyone else. We didn't help the kitchen people, however busy they were, and we certainly wouldn't help a housemaid.

The first, second and third housemaids were responsible for the appearance of the drawing room, and they made sure the curtains, chair covers, ornaments and flowers were in good order. They also saw that nothing needed dusting and that the furniture was kept well polished. The younger housemaids did the hard physical work of cleaning grates and laying fires.

As with housemaids, what a footman did depended on his rank. Generally, our first job in the morning was to wake the gentlemen and see that their clothes were brushed and laid out ready for them to wear. Later on we saw that the gentlemen's evening clothes were left clean and ready for them to step into for dinner. We laid the table for breakfast, lunch and dinner and cleared it afterwards. We served lunch and dinner. We laid the table for tea at four thirty in the afternoon and served drinks at six o'clock in the evening. Throughout most of the day—unless it was our morning for cleaning silver—we received guests, answered the telephone and waited on the family at the front of the house.

When dinner was over, we tidied the gentlemen's rooms and removed their clothes to brush them. At about ten thirty or eleven o'clock, there was the grog tray to take into the drawing room. And we weren't free until the family and their guests had gone to bed. If we were unlucky and they were playing a long game of billiards or cards, this might mean four in the morning. On really busy nights we didn't go to bed at all, as our day started again at six.

A footman wasn't given a free day. But as long as there wasn't a party, when everyone was expected to help, we were usually free every other day between lunch and dinner and after serving dinner. A wise man had a nap when he was off duty after lunch, because as soon as dinner was over he was going out.

In Ireland about forty or fifty of us met to dance square dances at the crossroads near Dunsany. We had nowhere else to go, as there wasn't a village hall within miles, but with four roads meeting we had quite a bit of space. We were lit by our bicycle lamps and by the light of the moon, and the Irishmen played accordions and fiddles. When it was over, the boys went behind one hedge to change into their working clothes, and the girls changed behind the other hedge. Then everybody disappeared to start work.

On a Saturday night in London we went to the Chelsea town hall, and in the country we usually went to a dance held in the village hall or the local town hall. The charleston was replacing square dances, and there'd be a five- or six-piece band playing. When I was valet to the second lord, we went by boat from the Mount to the mainland. Then we made our way to the town hall to dance. It was at one of these dances that I first met Barbara, before she became parlormaid at the Mount. She was staying on the island with John, the Mount postman, who asked if she could travel in the same boat with me to the dance. "Yes," I said. "But I hope she doesn't expect me to dance with her all night, because I'm simply not going to. Although if she likes to wait, I'll see that she gets back safely." I hadn't realized then that that would be the end of me!

When I accompanied the second lord on a weekend away, we rarely stayed in any house for longer than three nights. Even so, he traveled with at least three cases as well as his dressing case, all of which were my responsibility. We generally left home Friday morning and arrived in time for tea that afternoon. The weekend finished on Monday and we left immediately after breakfast, unless it was a weekend's shooting. Then he would shoot on Monday and we would leave on Tuesday.

Staff accepted me as a visiting valet, but they rarely had time for me because they had extra work looking after all the guests. And even where there was an enormous staff, as there was at Chatsworth, I was still more or less ignored, because when the duke had twenty to thirty guests staying, each guest demanded absolute attention. I always had an uncomfortable feeling that I was in the way wherever we were staying. I preferred shooting weekends because there was more for me to do. I was out all day loading for His Lordship, and then I had both sets of our clothes to clean when I returned. If there was another visiting valet staying, it was different. If we couldn't help out in the house, we could both go to the pub for a couple of pints and a game of darts.

A valet is neither up nor down. He is so close to his employer that other servants are wary of him. I had to be very careful as to what I said and how I behaved. Even at home I had to be on my dignity and most discreet–more discreet than the butler, because I was always with my employer and he would tell me things off the cuff. And although the first footman was likely to be very near a valet's own age and was probably a friend, the valet had to maintain a careful distance. The valet didn't eat with the first footman but with the older staff–the housekeeper, lady's maid and butler–in the housekeeper's room or steward's room.

A valet was a very lonely person. Even when I traveled abroad with the family party, I felt alone. Everyone aboard ship knew that I was a servant; the odd passenger might speak to me in the hopes this would lead him to my employer.

Civil servants were the worst. The ones I met were the most awful snobs. Once, when we were coming back from East Africa, a civil servant returning home on leave didn't see why I–a servant– should have a first-class cabin all to myself when he was in with three others. So I invited him in with me, although as soon as he arrived I realized my mistake. He began laying down the law at once and became so intolerable that I told His Lordship. In no time at all His Lordship saw the purser, and the civil servant was out of my cabin. He never spoke to me again for the rest of the trip!

On shipboard I was always friends with the crew. There was the bartender, the librarian and deck stewards to talk to. But we had little in common; they weren't in my line of business, and we didn't share the same interests in sport. Also, I had to stay aloof; if I had been the least bit brash, His Lordship would have wondered about me.

When we traveled abroad, I warned the station beforehand that there would be twenty or thirty pieces of luggage, including six specially made trunks, to be registered. I brought the luggage to the station at nine in the morning, and the next time I saw it was at Marseilles, where our ship was docked. Then all I had to do was stand at the gangway and allot it to the right cabins.

I never traveled alone with His Lordship. There was usually his sister, his brother and his daughter, as well as a lady's maid, and a registered nurse in case someone fell ill. We usually had the same nurse and I was company for her. On one trip she nearly married some scoundrel in East Africa. I asked her one day where her gold watch was, and she said she had given it to this man as a keepsake. I told her she was absolutely mad and that he was an out-and-out rogue. I was twenty-three at the time and she was in her forties, but I recovered her watch from him.

It was part of my job to see that His Lordship had every comfort when we arrived at a hotel. The trick is to ask the right people politely, and they are the people who supply things, not necessarily the manager. I would see the floor linen keeper about towels and soap and the chambermaid about where His Lordship wanted to have his bed and what he wanted moved in his room. Then I saw the floor waiters to make sure he would have the breakfast he wanted, and not what they thought he ought to have.

In one hotel I had trouble ordering His Lordship a cooked breakfast, which he preferred, as their usual breakfast was a continental breakfast. So I went down to the kitchen and told them I wanted two fried eggs on a plate. "There's no use telling me you don't do it," I said, "or I'll come and do it myself." And after that we got what we wanted.

We always went abroad as soon as Christmas was over. We'd leave about the second week in January and stay away until April. Most of the younger staff who were left behind took temporary jobs over that period. But they could have chosen to be put on board wages instead. This meant their keep would be paid for in addition to their wages, and in return they looked after the house.

A household was generally in London for the London season from May through July. Then we went to Scotland in August for grouse shooting and returned to London for the "little season," which was in September and October. Where you happened to be really depended on where the family's interests lay. When I worked for Lord Dunsany, we always returned to Ireland in August for the Dublin Horse Show, instead of going to Scotland to shoot grouse. Then we came back to London for the "little season."

Men's and women's quarters were kept strictly apart in every house with a staff of any size. Before a man could get anywhere near women's rooms, he had to pass the housekeeper, who was always on the watch. In the country the housemaids, stillroom maids and kitchen maids each had their own sitting room, which we were never allowed to enter. And they only went into each other's rooms if they were invited in and the housekeeper gave her permission. In London there weren't all these spare rooms, and everyone was either working or sleeping or had gone out.

The first footman always guarded the silver in both the London and country houses; he slept in the pantry, often across the door to the strongroom where the silver was kept. His was a foldaway bed, but most of the staff slept on hospital beds with straw or horsehair mattresses.

Every house had a servants' hall, which in my early days was only used at mealtimes. There was nothing comfortable about that room; it was painted a drab color and there was no carpet on the wood or stone floor. The only furniture was a long wooden table with a couple of benches either side of it, and a tall cupboard to keep the tableware.

The butler and footmen were always in the pantry. The best pantries had an adjoining office for the butler where he could write up his inventories. A butler was invariably married and nearly always went home after work, but at busy times he'd sleep overnight in his office. Most pantries had good natural light, and there was always a fire burning in the grate. They usually had wood floors and fairly high ceilings. Ideally they were large enough to hold four working men as well as a wooden table ten feet long by four feet wide. A wooden table was a blessing, because if we were in a hurry and put our trays down quickly, they didn't slide. We had two or three high stools instead of chairs, so when we sat down our coattails could pop down each side without becoming creased. The stools also served as stepladders to reach the top shelves.

The pantry bucket with its scrubbing cloths was kept under the sink, and the clothes basket and trays in a cupboard beside it. Generally there were two sinks with hot and cold running water. And in the courtyard outside was a rainwater tub, holding anything up to a hundred gallons. After it was filtered we used it for our washing, because rainwater is remarkably soft.

As a rule the only thing to separate the pantry from the front of the house was one baize door, which fit snugly and shut quietly. The pantry was in effect between upstairs and downstairs. There was a dividing line understood and recognized throughout the house. Everyone knew his or her place. We would never walk through the front of the house unless we were in uniform on business, and the gentleman or the lady of the house would never walk through the staff rooms without warning us first.

After the war most people were unable to afford the same amount of staff. I saw great changes in service as our people's life-styles became less grand. In my youth the butler was always available if the family needed him; otherwise, he merely supervised the staff. He had worked hard all his life, and he wasn't going to continue if he could help it! A butler in the old days would never have dreamed of doing as much day-to-day work as I did. He wouldn't have cleaned the silver, laid the table or seen to it that the reception rooms were orderly–those jobs belonged to the first footman. Nor did any of my staff wait on me as they would have done on a butler in the past.

Because my footmen worked their way up, I had to teach them everything from the very beginning. But I take great pride in the fact that almost all of the footmen I trained have gone on to work as butlers in private houses or in embassies abroad (including Washington D.C.), or to work for royalty.

RUNNING THE HOME

The three most important qualities for running a home are punctuality, organization and cleanliness. If you master these, everything else should fall into place. For me the first step in running a house is to get up early and leisurely in the morning, as I believe in letting the day come to me rather than rushing about with the day. My way I start out with a contented mind, rather than one that is in a state of confusion and unable to plan ahead.

PLANS AND SCHEDULES

In the great houses the butler and the lady of the house always planned everything together. At the Mount everything went through Her Ladyship first. I never did anything without consulting her, and she also asked my opinion. We met in her study every morning at ten o'clock to discuss the day's arrangements, which could take from five minutes to half an hour. She told me what each member of the family would be doing and what cars needed to be ordered— for whom and at what time. I was informed how many people would be having lunch or dinner and if guests were invited. If anyone important was coming, we discussed the menu, and I was told what provisions to order if people were coming to stay. Then it was up to me to relay the instructions to the footmen and the rest of the staff.

My orders didn't end with the morning meeting. I was asked to make arrangements for everything throughout the day, down to the smallest detail.

Fortunately my memory is so well trained that I never have to write anything down. Just as I could go into a room and see at once if anything was out of place, if an ashtray needed emptying or a cushion wanted straightening, so I could remember every order I was given without making a note of it. It was the same thing with telephone numbers; I knew every single one of them, even numbers from houses I had left long before.

RECORDS

Ordering and receiving provisions from the mainland for the castle was a complicated task. The fact that the castle is not only on an island but also on top of a hill made delivery doubly awkward, and coordination and cooperation were essential. On the mainland a chauffeur or tradesman had to stand on a jetty to guard the provisions until a boatman arrived. Then the shopping was brought over to the Mount and given to the engineer, who loaded it into the tram and sent it up to the castle. The tram is a wheeled bin that is hauled along an underground track on wire ropes up to the summit. When the tram arrived at the top, the youngest footman had to be there to take the provisions to the kitchen or the pantry.

For most people, written records of various kinds are very useful in running a household. As an example, it is a good idea to keep track of your groceries with an ongoing list. Everyone in the house can write on it whenever foodstuffs or household effects are required. Unless you have time to keep checking your store cupboard, as the housekeeper and cook did in the old days, you don't realize how low your provisions are becoming. Take your list along when you go shopping–you may think you will remember everything when you leave the house, but more often than not people don't.

Anybody who is at all busy should have an engagement diary. You can't remember everything, and it's terrible to forget appointments. If you keep a desk diary and look at it every morning, it keeps you up to scratch, and if you are away from your desk, and someone needs to know where you are, all they need do is consult your desk diary.

INVENTORIES

I also think it's wise to have a record of the valuables in your house for insurance purposes. All you need write is a description of the piece, the date it was bought and the cost. If it was a gift, write the approximate value and the name of the person who gave it to you. In the large houses a record was kept of everything. The lady of the house had a catalogue of the pictures and separate records for silver, china, glass and linen. The butler also had a record of the silver. Every item was listed and the inventories were checked at least once a year.

When I wrote out the silver inventory, I wrote a brief description of each piece with the year it was made–"George III epergne, 1761." The price wasn't recorded because someone came and appraised the silver each year for insurance purposes. I would advise anyone who has a considerable amount of silver to keep a similar book and to have the silver appraised yearly. If you have only a few bits and pieces you can do as Barbara and I do and note it in your household inventory, with a description of each piece and the appraisal value or the cost at the time of purchase.

A large house always had a wine record book. It was kept by the butler, because looking after the wine was one of his main responsibilities. Anyone who has more than two dozen bottles of wine should keep a similar record. Then you know immediately when you come to the end of one of your favorite wines, and you don't have to keep checking through your cellar to find out what you have left. If you are interested in wine, you should keep a book showing which wines you like and what they cost, so that you know what wines to buy and whether or not the price is right when you come to buy another bottle.

Either buy a special wine record book or make your own. This is very easy to do. Buy a hard-covered book with lined pages, and allow a double page for each specific wine or each case of wine. There are seven basic points of information that need to be recorded to give you a full understanding of the wine you have bought and tasted. And you should leave a space for your personal evaluation.

Wine		Sweet or Dry		
Wine Maker or Shipper				
Merchant/Date	Vintage	Price	Use Date/Remarks	

HOUSEHOLD ROUTINE

If I didn't have such a good memory, I would keep a list of the things I had to do each day (i.e., "return library book") and what I needed to buy. At the end of the day I would cross off what I had accomplished and make a fresh list for the next day.

The essence of household management is routine. Certain tasks must be done regularly to keep things up to standard. In my day we had specific times when specific things had to be done; everyone knew that pewter was polished on a certain day. If you are running a household without a staff, you might write up a schedule for routine tasks such as polishing furniture and cleaning silver. If the appearance of your possessions does not let you know that it is time to care for them, your calendar will.

CLEANING AND POLISHING

Polishing reflects the care put into natural wood, and a regular polishing with an aerosol such as Pledge or a wax polish such as Antiquax is the ideal way to bring up a shine. When you first polish a piece, use wax polish, so you know it has been conditioned. Then use wax and aerosol alternately until you have polished it to perfection and it is in perfect condition. After that you should use an aerosol frequently and try to wax polish once a month, or never less than four times a year.

TO POLISH FURNITURE

Aerosol polishes are easy and quick to use and don't require old-fashioned elbow grease. They contain chemicals that dry into a hard shiny film and form a protective layer. You spray the polish on, it dries instantly and you wipe it off with a clean cloth. Aerosol polish is ideal for brightening varnished pieces, as wax cannot penetrate their glossy coat.

Wax polish feeds and conditions wood. This is particularly important in winter, because central heating dries out wood furniture. Unlike aerosol polish, wax polish must be rubbed, and it takes longer to bring up a shine. It is solid and generally comes in a tin (although you can now buy Antiquax spray).

BARBARA'S WAX POLISH: The housemaids used to make their own polish, with beeswax, and Barbara makes an excellent wax polish. To make this polish, you need two ounces of beeswax, one dessertspoon of turpentine and one tablespoon of wine vinegar.

Beeswax is as hard as soap and must be melted. To do this, put the beeswax in an enameled bowl, place it in a saucepan of hot water on a low heat and stir. As the beeswax becomes malleable, carefully add the turpentine, which is very inflammable, and blend well. Then stir in the vinegar. Stir the ingredients very gently to avoid splashes that might ignite. Heat until the mixture becomes a smooth liquid. Then pour into a screw-top jar and seal it well. Barbara covered open jars with parchment, which she firmly tied with string round the jar. If you are using a screw-top jar, seal the lid with tape to keep the air out. Then store in a cool place.

POLISHING CLOTHS: For wax polishing you need three soft cloths: one cloth for applying the polish, one to give it a first shine and one to finish off with. Start by putting a small amount of polish on your putter-onner. I dislike seeing furniture crusted with polish or with bits of polish left behind in the swags, which shows that too much has been used. And if you polish furniture regularly over a period of time, only the smallest amount of polish is needed to make it shine. So don't dip or scoop your cloth into the tin or jar, but drag it across the top so you can scrape off any excess polish on the side. Then rub it over the surface. Rub again with the second cloth until the wood is no longer sticky. With a light circular motion, polish with the third cloth.

You can remove fingermarks and rings with wax polish. You need only a small amount of polish. Concentrate on rubbing it hard into the mark; you'll be surprised at how much will come off.

If I tell you our polishing cloths were old underclothes you won't believe it, but it's true! The best ones were made of silk and/or soft wool, and they never scratched. Furniture must be polished with soft cloths, the softer the better. Ladies' underclothes were best, as they were even softer and smoother than gentlemen's. Never throw away any cloth that's soft and won't scratch, as you never know when it might come in handy. Worn-out Viyella shirts, for instance, make superb polishing cloths.

Polishing cloths will become black if left unwashed, and the polish will be rubbed back into the surface when you try to put on a shine. I wash mine after every other time I use them. I don't bother to wash the cloth that applies the polish.

DUSTERS: To keep dust cloths soft–ideally they should be soft enough to polish glass–wash them with a mild detergent. Rub a little bar soap on and then rub the duster between your hands under the sudsy water. Give it a thorough rinsing, and let it dry naturally. Then rub the sides together to soften it. The housemaids washed their dusters every day, as their last job of the day.

Barbara runs the iron over our dusters–it makes them smoother, they pick up dust better, they don't scratch and they are never hard. Unironed dusters always have a touch of hardness and they remain slightly wrinkled. You should press dusters after you've switched off the iron, while you are waiting for it to cool down enough to store.

TO SCRUB A WOODEN TABLE

We always wiped a bare wooden tabletop after we used it. When we wanted to clean a table thoroughly, we scrubbed it. Before the first war tables were scrubbed with salt. Salt was used quite a bit one way and another. It came in a large block, which we broke up when we needed it, and we thought of it as rough common salt. Nowadays it's usually referred to as sea salt, and is expensive to buy because it has become known as a health salt. After the war we generally used scouring powder, which whitens wood more effectively than soap does. To scrub a table you will need a bucket and scrubbing brush, scouring powder or household soap and two cloths, one for rinsing and one for drying.

The scrubbing brushes you buy nowadays don't last five minutes. They become soft and mushy and the bristles fall out. But you must have a brush to do a good job of scrubbing, so buy the best you can find.

SCRUBBING: Always damp the surface before you begin scrubbing. This will make your soap or cleanser lather easily, which is important because lather lifts the dirt as it rises up through the water. Then wet your scrubbing brush so that it is fairly damp. Rub household bar soap onto it if you are using soap or sprinkle scouring powder on the table. If you sprinkle it directly onto the brush, it will fall in between the bristles. Some people would use half a tin and some very little. Personally, I would use very little indeed; about half a dessertspoonful is enough.

Never work up the grain on a wooden table. You must always work with the grain, from the top of the grain to the bottom, because the grain on wood, like the nap on cloth, must lie smoothly. Also, if you don't drag your cloth downwards when rinsing and drying, your fingers may pick up a splinter from a sharp edge that should have been lying flat.

Always change your scrubbing water when it becomes discolored and a scummy froth appears. After the table has been thoroughly scrubbed, empty out the dirty water and fill your bucket with fresh cold water for rinsing. Rinse with cold water because hot water would soften the wood whereas cold water helps seal it, whiten it and clean it. Use a cloth to remove the suds and absorb the water; it should be damp, not wet. Wipe it over the surface, return it to the bucket, squeeze out the water, damp it again—more than before—and continue rinsing until the wood is bright and shiny. Rinse well to avoid leaving white smears on the surface.

Take a dry cloth and roll it up tightly into a sausage. Drag it down the length of the table, pulling the water down the grain and into the bucket. Put a good deal of pressure on the cloth. To keep it straight, walk along by each side of the table; this will give you nice even lines like those you see on a Wimbledon lawn. Wring out your cloth and repeat until all the surplus water has been removed. A wooden table must always be left completely dry. If it isn't, over a period of time the top will become spongy, and you will no longer have a strong working surface.

An average-sized table can be washed, rinsed and dried in one go. But if your table is large, wash the top and then the bottom end, rinse and dry the whole table.

TO SCRUB A FLOOR

The best way to scrub a floor is on your hands and knees. I'd scrub any floor this way—stone, tile, linoleum or wood. I'm not a mop lover; a mop flicks water against the skirting board or splashes the furniture, which means extra work when you come to dry the floor. Also I don't think a floor ever looks clean of smears after being mopped. I think it's quicker and more hygienic in every way to scrub a floor on your hands and knees, as long as you have a kneeling pad to protect them.

You need a bucket of water with a drop of ammonia added, a scrubbing brush, household soap and two floorcloths.

Move the furniture out of the way and sweep the floor before you begin scrubbing. Always start at the wall farthest away from the door so you won't have to walk over your work when you have finished. Use a damp cloth to wipe as much of the floor as you can easily reach, which is about a square yard. Then damp your brush, rub soap onto it and scrub away, with the grain if you are scrubbing wood. Put pressure on your brush and work it into the area to remove dirty footmarks.

Damp your cloth in rinsing water to absorb the soap, wet it some more and continue rinsing. Dry the area thoroughly with your second cloth. Remember, the quicker the floor dries, the better–if someone comes in while it is wet and walks all over it, your work is ruined. Wash and dry each area before beginning the next; do one after the other until you have finished.

TO POLISH A FLOOR

Wood floors need polishing once a week. A machine will do this admirably. Polishing floors on your hands and knees is a warm job best reserved for a cold day, but it is a good way to wax. It is the only way you can get into the corners and along the skirting board.

You need one or two soft cloths for putting the polish on and bringing up a shine. Fold the first cloth into a pad and hold it in your right palm. Use a small amount of polish, as too much will make the surface sticky. Lean on your left hand and rub the polish in with your right hand, using a firm circular motion. To bring up the shine, you can either turn the pad back to front or use a second cloth. Use the same method as for putting the polish on, but exert less pressure. Never overreach yourself; each polished area should overlap the next. And don't polish the area under a small rug because someone standing on it might slide and fall.

TO MAKE FLOOR POLISH: You can make your own floor polish as follows. Cut half a pound of beeswax into fine strips and put it in an enameled bowl. As in making furniture polish, put the bowl in a saucepan of hot water and stir the beeswax over a gentle heat until it has melted. Then remove the bowl from the heat and add one and a half pints of turpentine. Blend well. Store in a well-sealed jar.

TO CLEAN LAMPSHADES

Lampshades become very dusty and should be brushed once a week with a soft, long-bristle brush. Brush downwards so as not to ruffle the nap. Brush the inside first.

TO CLEAN BOOKS

I respect books. I never turn down the top corner of a page. I can keep a book for thirty or forty years and it will be as good as the day I bought it. In the old days, when our people were away and we had time on our hands, we polished the covers and spines of their leather books. In the very large houses there was a librarian and a librarian's assistant whose job included doing this regularly.

POLISHING BINDINGS: To polish leather bindings you can use a very small amount of wax furniture polish. Put it on with a very soft cloth, rub it well into the leather and then polish up with the same cloth. Polishing gives a good shine that will sit on a leather book for a long time and make the spine slippery so the dust can't settle there. But it won't clean and preserve the binding.

CLEANING BINDINGS: Leather bindings do get dirty, but they should never be washed. Obstinate dirt can be removed with saddle soap. It is a good idea to test the soap on an inconspicuous part of the book first. It will probably darken all porous and light-colored leather bindings.

I put it on with a soft lint-free cloth, but you can also use a sponge. You mustn't put on too much, or it will leave a dark stain. Treat the leather very gently and don't rub too hard or you will wear it away. When you have finished, use a clean dry cloth—again, it should be soft—to remove all traces of soap.

CONDITIONING BINDINGS: Leather bindings should be conditioned every two or three years. I use a mixture of three parts neat's-foot oil to two parts anhydrous lanolin for this. I put the lanolin in an enameled bowl, then place it in a saucepan of simmering water. Lanolin can also be melted in the top half of a double boiler. After the lanolin has melted, remove it from the heat and stir in the neat's-foot oil with a wooden spoon. When the mixture has blended and cooled, I store it in a covered glass jar. It's always best to keep mixtures airtight if you are not going to use them immediately. I would seal the jar by putting cellophane tape between the lid and the glass.

It is best to put on this dressing a little at a time—if too much is used, it can bleed through the leather spine and onto the paper. I would rather apply several thin coats than put it all on at one go. Don't let the dressing fall on any part of the book other than the leather binding. If your book is half bound or three-quarters bound in leather and the rest of the binding is cloth, be extremely careful not to let the dressing get onto the cloth or it will leave a severe stain.

I make a pad of cheesecloth—you can also use cotton—to work the dressing into the leather. Clean the spine, headcaps, corners, edges and joints, as well as the back and front covers. There should be nothing hurried about this—steadily work the dressing into one area at a time. After the dressing has been absorbed, you should wipe off any excess with a clean piece of cheesecloth. Then lightly buff the surface to bring up a shine.

TO DUST BOOKS: I like to see books standing on the edge of a bookshelf. Nothing looks uglier than books pressed against a wall or the back of a bookcase. The spine of a book stored this way is hard to read, and it is difficult for air to circulate round the book.

Ideally books should be kept in temperate conditions, in an atmosphere which is neither too dry nor too hot—preferably between sixty and sixty-eight degrees Fahrenheit. Never store books

HOW STANLEY AGER DUSTS BOOKS

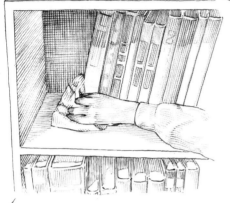

Dust is abrasive and should not be permitted to accumulate on fine bindings. Give your books and bookshelves a thorough dusting once a month. Take out the first four books at the end of a shelf and dust the space they have vacated with a duster or the nozzle of your vacuum cleaner. You now have enough room to move the rest of the books backwards and forwards. Push them back against the wall or to the back of the bookcase and dust the shelf in front of them. Then pull them out to the edge again, which is now dust free.

Tip three or four books towards you, and supporting them with your left hand, dust the tops of the pages and the spines with your right hand. Do this with groups of books until you reach the end of the shelf. Take out the last book and dust the exposed cover, then return it to its place. Lastly, dust the four books you removed, including the outside cover of the first book on the shelf, and replace them.

near a radiator. Also keep them out of direct sunlight, which will fade the bindings.

Dust is abrasive and should not be permitted to accumulate on fine bindings. Dust all your books once a week, with either the brushing attachment on the vacuum cleaner or an ordinary dust cloth. Hold your duster with the corners tucked in so they don't flap about and scatter the dust as you work. Start dusting on the top shelf and work downwards, paying particular attention to the spine and top edge of each book, where dust accumulates. The bottom edge is protected by the shelf and the front and back cover are protected by the books on either side.

TO MAINTAIN A CLOCK

All clocks should be treated with the greatest of care. Bearing in mind that a clock is often the most visible piece in a room, you should make sure it is kept immaculate. Dust your clock regularly, using a soft cloth so as not to scratch the glass protecting the face. If the glass becomes smudged or dirty, you may have to use a damp cloth to remove the marks. But be very certain to leave no moisture, because moisture can produce rust, which will play havoc with the works. Personally, I prefer to use a little bit of old soldier's breath–meaning I blow on the glass to moisten it. Then I use a chamois or duster for a brilliant shine.

If a clock's works need cleaning, I take it to a person whose trade it is. But there is a way of cleaning the works yourself which encourages a clock to keep time.

Dip a feather into paraffin, which Americans call kerosine, or into a Swiss-made clock oil. It is the fumes that do the trick, not the liquid itself–in fact, if any liquid fell onto the works, it would clog them up–so take only a tiny amount on the feather. Now open up the back of the clock and touch the works very lightly with the feather. Let the feather touch every wheel and spindle in turn, but do not allow it to touch the hairspring. This is a wire coil as fine as a hair which sits above the balance. If oil gets onto it, the coil will stick and the clock will run away with itself.

TO MAINTAIN A WATCH

A watch is too small to take kerosine from a feather, so if your watch is losing time, remove the back and put it next to a thimbleful of kerosine under a wineglass. Any dome-shaped glass will do, and the liquid can be left in an eggcup or bottle top instead of a thimble. This is a slow process; it takes a day to work. The glass seals in the fumes, which the watch absorbs.

Another good way to clean a watch and to make it go faster is to remove the back and put in a small piece of blotting paper that has been damped in paraffin. Replace the back and leave the watch face up overnight. When you open it again next morning, the dirt will have been absorbed by the blotting paper. But don't remove the back unless you know how to put it together again!

TO CLEAN A CHANDELIER

I looked after the large chandeliers that had been in the family for years. They had to be dusted on special occasions, to make sure there were no cobwebs hanging off the arms, and cleaned twice a year. I dusted them with a Turk's head–an old-fashioned chandelier brush. It looked like a soldier's busby on the end of a pole. I'd take a ladder–I don't trust chairs–and move it all the way around the chandelier, lightly dusting each arm in turn, taking great care not to knock off any crystal drops.

A chandelier should be cleaned at the start of every autumn and every spring. Flies are at work all summer, and during the winter months your fire may smoke, leaving soot and dust in the room. If the sun shines directly into the room and onto the chandelier, it will look ghastly if it's dirty. Washing chandeliers is a much more thorough way of cleaning them than using a commercial cleaner. Have a dust sheet to protect the floor and a bucket of sudsy water handy. I added half a capful of ammonia and a tablespoon of detergent to the water, bearing in mind that too much soap makes glass cloudy and sticky. For cleaning, I always used worn napkins. Old linen is ideal because it doesn't leave bits and pieces behind to catch in the chandelier and perhaps pull a drop from its pin. You need only a small cloth. A tea towel, for instance, would be too large and cumbersome.

Cleaning a chandelier is rather like milking a cow. It has the same rhythmic movement–you wipe, you polish, you wipe, you polish. You hold a damp soapy cloth in one hand and a dry cloth in the other. After washing a few drops, rub them with the dry cloth, rinse the soapy cloth in the bucket–it's quite incredible how much dirt will come away–then squeeze it free of water and wash a few more. Then you go onto the next and the next until you have cleaned them all. It doesn't matter how big your chandelier is, you must concentrate on each drop individually. Even so, the actual cleaning takes no time at all–most of the time is spent moving your ladder.

In order to avoid missing a crystal drop or even redoing any of your work by mistake, mark your starting point with a piece of paper or string. Begin at the top and work downward, tier by tier. If you started at the bottom and dropped something wet from the top, it would ruin the work you had already done.

Crystal drops must be handled lightly and gently because they are easily dislodged. Each is suspended from the frame by just one thin pin, which can easily become bent or worn. Look for these details when you wash your chandelier so that pins can be replaced if necessary; examining each drop will require very good eyesight and a tremendous amount of patience. Ideally you should have a few spare drops. Drops are rarely lost when you're actually cleaning a chandelier. In the old days breakages were much more likely to happen when a housemaid was using a broom to sweep the floor and the handle hit the chandelier.

TO CLEAN COPPER

For the life of me I don't know why copper was always used in kitchens. It made a tremendous amount of work; it would take two or three girls all day to clean all of it.

In my day kitchen coppers–pots and pans–were cleaned with malt vinegar and silver sand, which we bought by the hundredweight. The kitchen mixed half a cup each of silver sand and malt vinegar together to make a creamy paste. They used two soft cloths, one to apply and one to shine. We used this mixture on untreated copper. I wouldn't recommend using it on today's treated copper, for it will become streaky.

Brasso is an excellent copper cleaner and you can wipe treated copper with a damp cloth.

TO CLEAN PEWTER

You can use commercial brass or silver polish, or make your own pewter polish with methylated spirits and whiting if you can find it.

To make pewter polish blend equal parts of methylated spirits and whiting together to form a creamy paste, as thick as double cream. Apply the paste to your pewter with your fingers or a cloth. The amount you can take on the end of one finger is enough to polish a pint pot. Rub it in hard, then take a clean piece of cloth to bring up the shine. You could use a chamois to bring up more of a shine, but you will never get the same finish as on silver, which takes a much smoother and deeper shine. If you are cleaning eating utensils, wash them before storing.

TO CLEAN BRASS

Brass should be cleaned with a commercial brass polish. It should be cleaned as soon as it gets tarnished—on damp days and in damp conditions this means every twenty-four hours. Brass doorknobs, which are constantly touched by warm moist hands, must be cleaned every day. Four doorknobs can be polished in five minutes.

I always told my staff that if our doorknobs weren't highly polished and the income tax people paid us a surprise visit, they would think they were gold and not brass!

You need two cloths, one for putting the polish on and one for shining the brass. You need very little polish and you need to be brisk. Holding the polish bottle upright with your cloth over the top, give it a quick shake, and enough polish will be left on the lip. Never pour polish straight onto a cloth; if you have too much it

will smear the surface and make extra work.

Make a pad out of one cloth, hold it in your left palm and rub on the polish with it. Hold the other cloth loosely in your right hand ready to polish. Embossed parts need to be brushed, and an old toothbrush is excellent for picking out any polish that sticks inside.

For a quick shine use old soldier's breath–blow on it–which will leave enough moisture to create the friction needed for polishing. A touch of old soldier's breath always came in handy when we were pushed. It's quite surprising what a little bit of breath and a handkerchief will do. You could keep all brass shining by blowing on it, but you would look a bit silly bending and blowing on doorknobs and fenders!

TO POLISH STEEL FIRE IRONS

In the past we cleaned our steel fenders and steel fire irons with wood or coal ash,which is fine and powdery. It resembled scouring powder, only it was gray. Scouring powder would be the modern equivalent.

To clean fire irons, I make a pad out of an old rag, damp it and sprinkle on a teaspoon of scouring powder. I hold a fire iron in my left hand. This rubbing action is what removes the black, so the harder you rub, the better. When the steel shows through again, I dry the iron with an old duster and perhaps polish it up with another old duster kept specifically for this purpose. No duster–for that matter, no piece of cleaning equipment–should be used for two different types of cleaning tasks.

CHIMNEY BLACK: We have our chimney swept in autumn, at Christmas and in the spring. In between times we occasionally sprinkle a dessertspoon of sea salt into our fire, which helps to remove the black off the chimney and helps disperse the soot. Salt will also damp your fire if it starts to smoke; to deal with a smoky fire, throw several handfuls of sea salt on the flames.

Many of the rooms in the large country houses were heated by coal fires, and the thick walls helped keep the heat in. Hot water pipes ran through the first bedroom I ever had and they kept it lovely and warm. But the passages were like icy caverns. Hanging along these icy caverns were great hams all black with age. They hung outside the kitchen and stretched towards the pantry. When the hams arrived from the farm on the estate, the cook pickled them in brine and then put them in muslin bags, before hooking them onto the ceiling. About three years later they would be taken down, marinated and cooked. The day I began as a hallboy, I entered the house through the kitchen door. Above all the cooking smells, I remember most vividly the smell of these hams.

TO CLEAN SILVER

I learnt to clean silver by working on odd pieces and on the staff eating irons, as we called our cutlery. At first I cleaned the silver plate for the steward's room. Most lads cleaned the staff silver with plate powder, and under duress. But I used silversmiths' rouge, which was ordinarily used on only the best pieces, and I rubbed it in with my fingers. I wanted the silver in the steward's room to look as good as the silver in the dining room. I had some soup-spoons to do which came up quite lovely, and I remember one of the valets saying, "You've done an excellent job with these!" I took pride in that remark. And from that moment I've been interested in cleaning silver.

In my day a couple of footmen spent three hours in the pantry every morning cleaning silver. They cleaned all the pieces that had been used the day before and any pieces that appeared tarnished. After a party everything was cleaned, and the pieces that weren't in general use were wrapped in tissue paper and stored ready for the next occasion.

The more you clean silver, the greater the reward. Our silver was brought up to a very high standard because we cleaned it so often. Most people cannot clean their silver every day, as we did, but you should look over your silver once a month and clean any pieces that are tarnished. Silver needs more care in winter because there is more smoke in the air, and smoke causes tarnish. There is smoke from log and coal fires, and windows are left shut, so if people smoke, a room becomes fuggy. Before London became a smokeless zone, where only smokeless fuel is allowed, silver turned yellow or tarnished in one day. In houses without a large staff, a silversmith came and lacquered the silver every six months.

POLISHES: We used silversmiths' rouge, which was mixed with water to a creamy consistency. Then we added one part plate powder to two parts rouge. The plate powder kept the silver from becoming dark, and the rouge gave it a deep shine rather than a white look. The rouge contained red oxide of iron, and when we rubbed it in very hard with our fingers, which created friction and warmed the silver so that it was malleable, it actually filled in the scratches.

Sadly, rouge is no longer readily available. But there are plenty of other things on the market that do a decent job. Today, I use a creamy liquid polish that is completely nonabrasive. Any liquid cream polish is most likely as good. It won't fill in scratches, as rouge did, or give silver quite the same luster. But if you use it correctly, you will be left with what, these days, amounts to an unsurpassed shine.

CLOTHS: You need two soft cloths. The first is for putting on the polish; it should be folded two or three times. The second is for bringing up the shine. Some polishes require to be put on with a damp cloth, which I think is better than using a moist sponge. For a truly deep shine—and this is something that not everyone knows—you should finish off all silver by rubbing it with a chamois leather. But it must be a genuine animal skin and not a simulated chamois. I wash my chamois about once a year when it seems to have absorbed too much silver polish and is beginning to look gray. (To wash a chamois so that it will stay soft for years, see page 90.)

BRUSHES: I use a soft natural bristle nailbrush or old toothbrush to remove bits of dried polish from the crevices of embossed work. Soft toothbrushes are especially handy for heavy embossing. I would always save them whenever I had a chance. Her Ladyship used to recognize hers when she came into the pantry. She'd say, "That's my toothbrush!" And I'd reply, "It *was* your toothbrush. Now it's my silver brush."

After brushing the polish from the crevices, I lightly brush the embossed work with a second brush to remove all traces of polish and bring up the first shine. Our second brushes were special silver brushes. Those without handles were called "flat backs" and were used for brushing larger surfaces, such as the beaded edge of a coffee tray. The ones with handles are still available today. We described them by how many rows of bristles they had, ranging from six (a "sixer") to one (a "one-er"). The most common type had either three or four rows of bristles.

Properly maintained, a silver brush can easily last your lifetime. Some of the silver brushes at the Mount dated from the nineteenth century. The secret lies in the care and cleaning. We never washed our brushes in water; we dusted them with whiting and then brushed them on newspaper. You cannot use this method today because the newsprint would come off on the bristles and you cannot easily buy whiting. Instead, use strong white shelf paper. Wrap it round an edge of a table, and then rub the brush up and down it from one end to the other.

TO REMOVE FOOD STAINS: Always wash silver as soon as possible after using it to avoid stains and dried food particles. Never leave sauces in sauceboats or a silver spoon in a mustard pot or salt cellar. Salt should never be left in silver, as it attracts damp.

Egg stains turn silver blue, grouse stains turn silver all colors and gravy that contains garlic can stain it. I have found Goddard's Silver Dip excellent for removing these stains, and Goddard's Long Term Silver Foam is best for removing green vegetable marks from dishes.

TO REMOVE WAX FROM SILVER: Never scrape wax from silver candlesticks and never immerse them in water, which would wet the baize or felt on the bottom. Wet baize will rot; also, if you set damp baize on a polished table, it will make a mark on the finish.

The right way is to put your silver candlesticks on the draining board and pour very hot water directly on them from a jug. Hold the candlestick up at an angle and let the water run down towards the base; be sure to keep the baize dry. The very hot water will remove all surface wax from the candlestick, but there will still be some residue of wax and grease. In fact, there will be grease whether or not there's wax, because you've been handling the candlestick and your hands are greasy. So wipe the candlestick with a damp cloth and dry it with a tea towel before you start polishing.

If by chance you do get the baize wet, you must get it dry–by putting it near heat or standing it out in the sun–before you can use the candlestick again.

TO REMOVE DAMP SPOTS: Silver that is kept in a damp place usually develops a smell and can become black or spotted. I will never forget unwrapping the silver epergne at the Mount. I wanted to have it in fine condition for the Princess Royal's forth-coming visit, but it had been stored for thirteen years in baize bags, which had attracted the damp. It took me three months of daily cleaning to eliminate the odor and bring the look back up to standard, and we had it out on the table when she came.

If your silver has been affected by damp, you must first of all remove the smell. To do this, wash the piece in a gallon of warm water with two teaspoons of mild detergent and half a capful of ammonia (with no color or additional fragrance) added. It may take two or three washings before you are satisfied that the smell has gone. Then rinse the piece a couple of times under hot–not boiling–water to allow it to dry quickly.

Wipe off any black or spotted parts with silver polish. Use an old duster, as it will be as black as ink by the time you have finished and ready to throw away. Wash the piece again, then leave it to air. The next day look at it and smell it. If any odor remains, wash and clean it once more. Otherwise start applying silver polish to work up a shine.

Silver is malleable and responsive and soon comes back to a fine condition. And after two or three days of regular cleaning, you will be delighted at the difference–your piece will resemble silver again instead of a bit of old iron!

PICKING UP SILVER

Silver will need less frequent cleaning if you avoid leaving finger-marks on it. The trick is to pick up a piece of silver by an edge and then support it from underneath, never touching the face or major surfaces.

Pick up bowls and candlesticks as gingerly as you can. I pick up a candlestick by its rim or its shoulder, the section between the rim and the middle. If a bowl has no handles, I tip it forwards so that I can slip my fingers underneath and pull the base onto the palm of my hand. I support a small bowl by resting my thumb on the rim. I avoid marking a bowl when putting it down by placing it the same way I place a dish or plate (see page 146).

HOW TO POLISH SILVER

Before you start, cover the cleaning surface to protect it. We put baize over our wooden tables to keep the rouge from getting on our tabletops. The baize also prevented the scouring powder, with which the table had been cleaned, from getting on our silver. This was particularly important because scouring powder is an abrasive. Make sure your silver is properly washed and free from grease (see page 157).

I put only a small amount of polish on my first cloth, then I rub it in briskly until it disappears. The friction will rub out stains and produce a shine that will make any scratches appear less obvious. There's no hard and fast rule, but I generally work with the first two fingers of my right hand against the cloth, unless I'm cleaning a large piece, when I use my first three fingers. I keep on rubbing until the silver becomes quite warm. In the old days when we removed scratches by furiously rubbing rouge into them, my fingers and the silver became so hot that if I touched someone with a piece I was cleaning they would think they had been burnt.

You must hold the piece so that you are comfortable and you can see what you are doing. Take the first cloth in both hands with the piece resting on top of it; hold the piece steady in one hand and work the polish in with the other. Take care when rubbing polish into knife handles; I always hold the knife at the shoulder (between the blade and the handle) to avoid cutting myself.

If a piece is awkward to hold, I use the table for support. I do all my smaller trays, flat dishes and bowls this way. I steady the piece with my left hand and rub in the polish with my right hand. I tilt the piece towards the light so I know when I have rubbed in enough polish. I always clean and polish the inside of a bowl before I apply polish to the outside. To clean the outside, I hold the rim between my forefinger and thumb and tip the bowl backwards. Keeping it tilted, I push it round on its upturned base with my forefinger and thumb and rub in the polish with my free hand. Then I pick the piece up to polish and chamois.

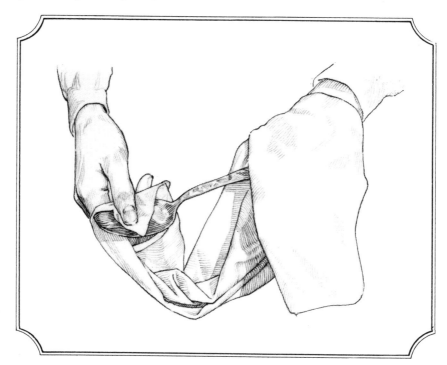

After I've rubbed polish into a piece, I work on the embossing with my two brushes. Either I continue using the table for support or I pick up the piece and hold it in one hand while brushing it with the other. Polish doesn't stick only in embossing. If I am cleaning a fork, I use my second brush to brush up and down the tines, as polish has a way of wedging itself between them. (Never brush across the tines, as this could scratch the silver.) To clean the feet on a tray or dish, I brush round the feet. Lastly, I brush where a handle is joined to a bowl, tray or dish.

Then I polish the entire surface with my polishing cloth. This must always be done gently. I pick up most items and rest them on my polishing cloth. If they are too large to hold and polish with the same cloth, I hold them with a spare cloth to avoid leaving finger-marks, then use my second cloth to polish.

The final touch is to polish with a chamois. This is basically a light, brisk drying action, never a hard rubbing motion.

TRAYS AND DISHES: Large heavy pieces will need to be laid flat on the table. I prefer to lay trays and dishes face down and work on the back first. If the piece has feet, I brush round the feet after applying the polish. After polishing and rubbing with the chamois I turn the piece over to do the front. I rest the center of a footed piece on a folded hand towel so that the feet are lifted off the table and are free of pressure. Then I clean the front.

CANDLESTICKS: To clean very tall candlesticks, those over fifteen inches high, I stand them on a table. I start at the top, rather than the base, so no polish can fall on the work I have already done. I hold the middle between my forefinger and thumb and turn the candlestick as I rub polish round the top with my free hand. Then I turn the top of the candlestick while I rub polish into the middle and the base. (You may want to hold the top with a spare cloth so as not to stain your hand with polish.) I repeat the exercise to polish and chamois.

CLOTHING CARE AND PACKING

When I fetched young Trotter from Eton, I would send him to the men's lavatory to wash before he came back with me, because Etonians, like most other boarding school boys, have an unclean, doggy smell clinging to them. In many ways a man remains a little boy–he likes to play with mud and doesn't mind becoming dirty! A woman is generally the complete opposite and takes trouble over her appearance. A well-turned-out person has well-brushed hair, clothes that are tidy and properly brushed and clean shoes. But personal hygiene is the pearl in the oyster of successful dressing and must be maintained at all times.

The frequency with which you change your shirt depends on how much you perspire and where you live. If you have perspiration problems, live in a city or commute to work, you should change your shirt every day. A woman changes her shirt far more often than a man–Barbara never wears a shirt twice.

You should bathe or shower every day and wash your hair as soon as it looks dirty. And you should have a bath or shower, and at the very least change into a clean shirt, if you are dining away from home. Neither of us would dream of going out in the evening without a bath and a complete change of clothes. The trick is to get ready fast. I can wash, shave and completely change in five minutes because my wardrobe is arranged so I know exactly where everything is. I always put my clothes back in the same place so I can locate anything I need in a hurry. You can save time by leaving your clothes for the evening neatly folded on a chair when you go to work, so they are ready to step into when you have bathed or showered on your return home. A man must always shave before he goes out in the evening, and a woman must apply fresh makeup.

If you are going out for the evening directly from work, wash as thoroughly as possible at the end of the day. Keep a sponge bag where you work, with a toothbrush, toothpaste or mouthwash (particularly important if you smoke), deodorant and talcum powder. Talcum powder is especially good for absorbing perspiration and is soothing on the feet (putting it between the toes helps prevent athlete's foot). I also put it on my face after shaving. A woman should have her makeup bag handy and a man should have a razor, as well as shaving cream for a safety razor, or preshave if he uses an electric razor.

A man who will not be returning home before an evening out should carry an extra clean handkerchief. The old one can be used during the day, and the clean one will be presentable for use in company. If you wear a handkerchief in your breast pocket it must be clean and remain untouched.

Put on a clean shirt in the morning so that it will still look reasonably fresh by evening. (A woman might prefer to take along a clean one in her briefcase or work bag. She might wear this shirt the next day if it was unmarked and she wasn't going out again.)

In my line of work we had to look immaculate no matter what. On a big party night I would go through as many as three or four stiff-fronted evening shirts. I would feel my shirt wilt as I became hot from running up and down stairs. I'd say to one of my footmen, "Right! I'm just going to change." Bathing was the best way to take away the perspiration, so I always left the bath half full of water. I would go straight in one end and out the other, and in five minutes I'd have a clean shirt on, brush my hair and be ready for work.

Wash your brushes and comb frequently to avoid rubbing dirt back onto your head when it's clean. Footmen no longer wore wigs when I started, but we did powder our hair. We were given powder money, but instead of buying powder we kept the money and pinched flour out of the kitchen to use instead!

I'll tell you a story about using hair powder. In London during the social season footmen went to one pub and butlers went to another. If a butler needed staff for a large party, he went to the footmen's pub and found someone who could be available that night. Our employers turned a blind eye to this system, because although they didn't like their servants to be hired out for the evening, they knew their butlers used it when it suited them.

On one particular night I was booked for the Albermarles' party. Lady Dunsany was at home and His Lordship was at his club. It was my night off, so I felt no one would miss me. At the Albermarles' my livery blended in nicely with everyone else's, and I was put inside the front hall to take the guests' coats. But while I was standing there, I suddenly caught sight of Lady Dunsany.

I went tearing into the dining room, where the butler was showing the cook how the table was laid.

"My lady's just arrived," I told him. "Seeing she's such a good friend, she must have been asked at the last minute because someone dropped out."

"Oh, my God!" he said. "What are we going to do? I must have you because Her Ladyship wants a double service!" This meant that both ends of the table were served at the same time, so one group of servants waited on the eight guests at the bottom while another group served the eight guests at the top.

Then he looked at me and said, "I know what we'll do. Go up and see Frederick—that's His Lordship's valet—and ask to borrow his tailcoat, which should just about fit you. Put some powder in your hair to change the color so she won't recognize you. You can serve the bottom of the table, and she'll be on the right of His Lordship at the top. After dinner, instead of serving coffee you can dash off home."

"Right!" I said.

So I served dinner and left as soon as it was over. When I arrived home, I told my second footman that I would wait up to open the door for Lady Dunsany and that he should go to bed.

Her Ladyship returned early. "I thought John was on duty tonight," she said.

"He was. He wasn't feeling very well, so I said I'd wait until Your Ladyship returned," I replied.

She gave me a very knowing look as she said good night. I didn't think much of it until later when I glanced in a mirror and saw I still had the powder in my hair. She knew.

BRUSHING

I have always enjoyed looking after clothes and been proud of the end result. I originally learnt clothes care by watching the valets at work. Lord Coventry's valet was the first; I worked for him when I began in service as a hallboy. Everything was brand-new to me. I had never been in a large country house before, and I saw chaps caring for clothes in a way that I had never imagined. I was always eager to learn, and I started by practicing on my own clothes.

The valet I learnt the most from was William Hammond, who later became butler to the Bishop of Birmingham. He was terrifically knowledgeable; he was excellent at cleaning hunting clothes and was also a superb silver cleaner. We both worked for Lady Barbara Smith.

Caring for clothes was an art in those days. We had a way of doing our work, particularly dull work, that people nowadays can't understand. Caring for clothes requires patience, and how do you learn the patience of anything? My footmen learnt by copying me. But if they weren't interested in their work, I wasn't interested in them. If they couldn't be bothered to learn, then I wouldn't waste my time teaching them.

Brushing is the first step in clothes care. All clothes look better for brushing, which restores their newness and freshens them up. And it removes dust, which is extremely important because dust is an abrasive and in time will wear on your cloth.

BRUSHING ROOMS

Most of the television programs I watch about life below stairs are rather misleading. For instance, on one program I saw a butler taking his gentleman's clothes through the kitchen. Well, we would never have taken any of our clothes anywhere near the kitchen or let one kitchen person lay a greasy eye on them. We took care of our clothes in special brushing rooms.

The valet's brushing room was usually separate from the footmen's brushing room, which adjoined the boot hall where the shoes were cleaned. In most country houses there were rooms to spare which a valet might take for his brushing room.

In the castle my brushing room was the footmen's bathroom. During the day it belonged solely to me. I had it adapted to suit my needs. The bath went out of action; a wooden lid came over the top of it, which I used as an ironing board.

Generally the door of a valet's brushing room could be shut and locked after he left. The door to the footmen's brushing room, however, was always open, as the room was in constant use. When a footman called his gentleman in the morning, he took away the evening clothes and put them in the brushing room to work on while his gentleman was at breakfast, and that was just the beginning. A footman carried his gentleman's clothes up and down, from the bedroom to the brushing room and back, all day long.

If a valet was forced to share a brushing room with the footmen, he was top of that brushing room. After all, he was older and more experienced than they were. He was very particular because his gentleman's clothes were his responsibility. If he was using the footmen's brushing room, none of the footmen would dare use any of his things—his brushes or his irons. That was just not allowed. If I had to share a brushing room, I always had my own corner, and nobody was allowed in it.

A brushing room was a utility room and looked exactly like one. There were no curtains or chairs, and the walls were whitewashed. By the time I started in service, most of the houses had electricity, so our rooms were well lit by electric light rather than the softer lamplight. Some of our rooms had ordinary plank floors; others had better floors with wooden blocks set into them, which were a more pronounced design than parquet. But whatever the floor was like, one of the younger boys or the odd-job man had to keep it scrubbed.

Ideally a brushing room had one jolly good table, a large one taking up the middle of the room so you could work on each side of it. Our table at Dunsany was approximately fifteen feet long and four feet wide, standing on eight solid legs. We had a couple of sinks with good-sized draining boards, to clean hunting clothes on, and a flat-topped stove where we heated the old-fashioned flatirons and kept them warm. Tall cupboards lined the walls. Each footman more or less had his own; he kept his heavy irons on the bottom shelf when they weren't on the stove, and his brushes handy on the first shelf. There were two wooden racks hanging on either side of the room. I had to hang my gentleman's clothes on them after we returned from traveling, and I kept his things there until I could work on them. None of his clothes were ever put away unless they were perfectly clean. I might work right through the night so that they were up to my standard and ready next morning.

HOW TO USE A BRUSH

It is the correct use of your clothes brush that really removes dust. Always remember that brushing should never be a scrubbing movement; it requires a strong sweeping motion or a firm flick of your wrist on areas where dust has accumulated. All strokes must go the same way; otherwise, when light strikes the cloth, it will look a mess, like the ruffled hair on a horse's shank.

You must first brush up the nap—i.e., brush against the lie of the material—to remove all the dust that is trapped inside it. Then brush down the nap for a smooth finish. If you want to brush out a mark, concentrate on brushing it with short, quick strokes, but never jab at cloth or you are likely to break the fiber.

You can freshen up your clothes by using a damp brush on them. Dip the bristles of your brush in a bowl of water (my bowl holds approximately one gallon) with a very small amount of ammonia added. Then flick the water from the bristles so your brush is left slightly damp, not wet, and brush as usual.

You should add to your water only enough ammonia to cover the bottom of the bottle cap. I say this because I remember quite distinctly being told by a first footman not to use too much ammonia when freshening up a dark suit. At first I had thought, "Oh, I'll add a drop more, it will clean it twice as quick." But he said, "If you do that on dark clothes, you'll turn them green."

I always brush evening clothes with a slightly damp brush. If a suit is very dusty, I first brush it with a dry brush, and then I use a slightly damp brush to freshen it up.

CLOTHES BRUSHES

Natural bristle clothes brushes are best of all. Synthetic bristles have less "give," and because they are hard, they can scratch the fabric. Also, synthetic bristles will wear out relatively quickly, whereas a natural bristle brush should last you a lifetime. My clothes brush is made by Kent of London. It is excellent and has lasted for more than forty years. Good brushes are, of course, expensive, but they are long-lasting.

To my mind, anyone who travels anywhere should take a small traveling clothes brush. I always carry a small natural bristle traveling brush with me whenever I go away. It fits handily into a suitcase.

A velvet-faced lint brush can be used on finely woven and soft materials and on men's evening clothes (i.e., a dinner jacket). This type of brush is ideal for picking up fluff, hair or clinging particles. Some people remove these little bits with tape, but I think this could leave marks on the fabric. It is best to remove them with your fingers, but this takes time and a great deal of patience. I used to swear like mad when the third lord had a dog on his lap during the course of an evening; it would take me ten or twenty minutes the next morning to pick the hairs off his suit with my fingers.

I clean my clothes brushes the same way I clean my shoe brushes and silver brushes. These brushes need only occasional cleaning, and this is the best method that I know of. I take a piece of strong white shelf paper or brown wrapping paper and wrap it round the edge of a table. I always double the brown wrapping paper and have the dull side (rather than the smoother side) face up. Then I take the brush and rub it briskly back and forth over the paper, from end to end.

BRUSHING TABLES

I like to brush on a table. An unfinished wooden table is excellent; I always wipe it with a damp cloth before and after use. A polished table is so slippery that you must put the garment on a blanket or a strip of baize so it will not slide about. In this case, remember to cover the blanket or baize with a sheet so no fluff comes off onto your garment.

You can brush on almost any flat surface, provided it is at waist level and large enough to spread out your garment on. The surface should be firm so that you can bring some pressure to bear on the brush. I find a bed is a little bit too soft. Also there's danger of fluff coming off the bedspread, which makes for extra work–a candlewick bedspread is the devil for this!

If you don't happen to be near a suitable brushing surface, you can brush a skirt or jacket on its hanger. You should use a wooden hanger, which is sturdier and easier to hold steady than a flimsy wire hanger. Hold the garment with one hand and brush with the other. You must hold the garment at arm's length so you can turn it and see what you are doing. Again, you must never brush blindly; all brush strokes must be in the same direction.

I once knew a very fussy film actor who had a bust of his own figure specially made so that when his clothes were brushed and pressed on it they would fit him perfectly. But I didn't think this was a good idea at all. I couldn't put any pressure on the brush, nor could I brush up the nap vigorously, because it felt like a person.

FABRICS AND GARMENTS

VELVET: I would never use a bristle brush on velvet, because it can mark the material. You should use a brush with a velvet finish on the face, or better still, a piece of velvet. Gently rub the piece of velvet down the nap of the velvet garment. Never rub up the nap, or you will leave a mark. Steaming is the best way to liven up velvet and should be done last thing; you can hang the garment in a steamy bathroom while you're taking a bath or shower before going out.

TWEED: You can kill a chicken very easily but you need much more force to kill an elephant. Wool tweed is stout and needs specially strong treatment. We used to brush tweed with a special stiff brush called a dandy brush, which had long straw bristles. I don't believe this type of brush is available anymore, but brushing vigorously up and down the nap with a regular clothes brush is just as effective a way to remove dust from tweed.

I feel that a well-tailored suit should be kept looking like one, whether it is a woman's suit or a man's. Tailored suits take three times as much care as casual suits. Closely woven twills and synthetics don't need much brushing because dust doesn't stick to them. But a wool or tweed suit should be brushed every time it is worn, either before or after wearing. It takes less than five minutes.

You should always brush a wool or tweed suit if you haven't worn it for some time. At the very least you should shake your suit before you put it away. A suit made of another fabric should be checked before every second wearing and brushed if necessary. Brush evening clothes much more gently than you would everyday clothes. And be careful when brushing a dinner jacket that the bristles don't scratch the silk facings.

TO BRUSH A JACKET: Take everything out of the pockets so that they lie flat and if they have flaps make sure the flaps are not tucked inside. Then turn up the collar and lapels before laying the jacket flat face downwards. Fold back the shoulders so they lie flat and the sleeves fall naturally on either side of the back seam.

Because I am right-handed I start from the right, which on a man's jacket is where the buttons are. Wherever you start, always brush up the nap first and then brush down the nap immediately afterwards. Brush the entire length with a single long stroke, which will allow you to be fairly vigorous and will leave no brush marks.

TO BRUSH TROUSERS: If your trousers have cuffs, turn them down before you start brushing. An incredible amount of dust collects there, because you kick dust into them as you walk. You must brush up the nap first to uncover the dust, and then smooth the nap by brushing downwards. Brush the dust out of the cuffs with short quick strokes. Next brush the outside of the leg from the cuff to the waistband in sweeping motions. Then brush down the nap from the waistband to the cuff. Turn the leg back and brush the inside of the opposite leg (including the material on both sides from the crotch to the waistband) with the same long brush strokes. Brush from the cuff to the waistband and from the waistband to the cuff.

Turn the trousers over and brush the outside of the second leg. Then pull back the second leg and brush the inside of the first leg.

If your trousers are cuffed, fold them back correctly. You now have a well-brushed pair of trousers.

HOW STANLEY AGER BRUSHES A JACKET

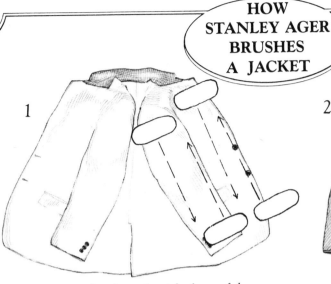

1

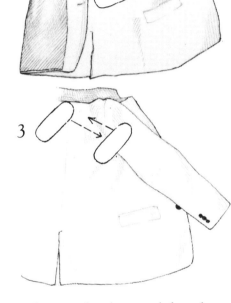

2

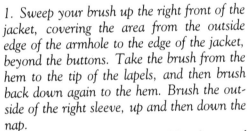

3

1. *Sweep your brush up the right front of the jacket, covering the area from the outside edge of the armhole to the edge of the jacket, beyond the buttons. Take the brush from the hem to the tip of the lapels, and then brush back down again to the hem. Brush the outside of the right sleeve, up and then down the nap.*

2. *Fold the sleeve forward and brush up and down the nap on the inside. Fold the sleeve back to its first position.*

3. *The shoulders are the next part of the jacket to brush. Take the brush from behind the outside of the shoulder to the inside edge of the collar, and then back again from the edge of the collar to the tip of the shoulder. Brush the shoulder using short quick strokes, because it is a small area. It is particularly important that the bristles of the brush lift the fibers of the material on the shoulder, as this is where dandruff collects and dust is most likely to accumulate.*

Next brush the left-hand side of the jacket, using the same strokes as you did on the right. Otherwise the garment would look patchy and uneven in the light. You then, of course, brush up and then down the nap. Brush the outside of the second (left) sleeve first, then fold it forward and brush the inside, not forgetting to brush the part of the jacket behind it. Fold it back to its first position and then brush the shoulder.

Do the collar last; brush across the interfacing from left to right and right to left. You will be surprised at the amount of dust that has collected there! Then fold the collar back down and brush forwards and backwards across it. Your jacket is ready to wear or to hang in your cupboard.

TO BRUSH A SKIRT: Lay the skirt flat on a table. Begin by brushing the back. Brush from the hem to the waistband, then smooth the nap by brushing from the waistband to the hem. Turn the skirt over. Always save the final brushing for the front of the skirt, as this is more visible.

TO BRUSH FELT HATS AND BOWLERS: You should brush a hat to remove settled dust after you take it off. I use a clothes brush on hats, but I brush gently so as not to finish with a bald patch, as there isn't a great deal of nap to play with.

TO BRUSH A FELT HAT

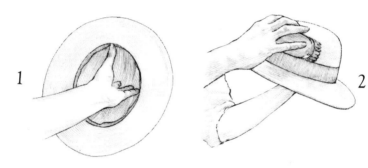

1. Place your left hand inside the crown with your palm turned upward. Press your thumb against the headband on one side and spread your fingers to steady the inside crown.
2. Now begin brushing in a clockwise direction, starting above the ribbon and working upwards to the top of the crown. As you work, turn the hat by rotating your left wrist anticlockwise. When you have brushed the crown, brush round the brim in exactly the same manner.

TO BRUSH A VELVET RIDING HAT: Place a riding hat near a boiling kettle and steam it, then brush it with a fine natural bristle clothes brush. Hold it as you would a bowler or felt hat, and smooth the nap by rotating your left wrist anticlockwise and brushing anticlockwise with your right hand.

CLEANING AND LAUNDERING

I'm attached to my old clothes because I don't have to look after them. But if clothes aren't cared for properly when new, they don't last to become old.

Barbara and I look after our own clothes better than any dry cleaner or laundry ever could. Only once in our married life have we used a laundry. We sent some blankets to what was then considered the best laundry in England, and they came back as stiff as a board! From that day on we have always done our own washing. If Barbara is unable to wash, I wash. Of course it is only because I have been looking after clothes all my life that I can go my own way. But I'm not opposed to your sending clothes to a dry cleaner or laundry if you prefer not to undertake the task yourself.

PROPER CARE

To look after your wardrobe properly it's important to know your clothes. You should read the labels to find out what kind of fabric they are made of and how to take care of them. If the label says "Dry clean only" you should do so. But if a label says a colored garment is colorfast, it is best to be a little disbelieving and wash it separately from white things. Even the slightest color bleed will affect the appearance of a white garment. Whether I'm washing by hand or by machine, I always sort clothes into two piles—one for colored things, and one for all-white garments. To make quite certain that coloreds don't run into each other, I put half a teaspoon of salt in the washing water. It works.

WATER: The secret of all washing is the water. Detergent lathers more easily in soft water than in hard. This means that if your water is soft you can use less detergent, so the clothes will need less rinsing. The softest, and I believe by far the best, water for hand washing is country rainwater that has been strained through gauze or fine linen. Because rainwater is so incredibly soft it brings up a wonderful lather when detergent is used with it. I know few people nowadays, if any, keep a supply of rainwater for washing. This was, however, commonplace when I was young. The up-to-date alternative to rainwater for hand washing is to add approximately four drops or one-third of a capful of household ammonia, which has no added color or fragrance, to two gallons of warm water. Use one-half of a capful if your water is hard. Although I've never seen ammonia sold as a water softener, it seems to do the trick; it's inexpensive and it has a variety of other uses. In a washing machine, however, you should use a commercial water softener.

DETERGENT: Although you need to maintain a good lather when machine washing clothes, hand washing, because of hearty scrubbing, requires very little detergent. Heavy use of detergent leads to more rinsing and extra work for you. You need just enough to cause the suds to bubble up through the cloth. This action releases the grease and dirt trapped in the fibers.

Barbara and I use commercial detergents. We use a mild detergent on delicate clothes (wool, silk and ladies' underclothes), a strong detergent on tougher fabrics such as cotton.

BLEACH: Be extremely careful with liquid chlorine bleach. It is very strong and can rapidly damage both your clothes and your skin. When it is mixed with some detergents or with ammonia a powerful chemical reaction may result, so always read the instructions on the labels of all products before combining them. Never pour bleach onto dry laundry, and remember that it's better to use too little rather than too much.

Whenever I plan to use chlorine bleach I test it first on an unnoticeable part of the garment. If the garment is made of a fiber blend I proceed as if it were made of the most delicate fiber, the one most likely to be hurt by chlorine bleach. When I wash a shirt made of cotton and polyester, for instance, I avoid using bleach. Polyester reacts badly to chlorine bleach, whereas most cottons do not. Don't use chlorine bleach on nylon or on completely synthetic fibers, and never use it on wool.

I remember receiving a telephone call from Colonel Trotter's son shortly after I left the Trotters. He said his best white wool hunting breeches had turned yellow, and he wanted to know why and what he could do about it. "They're bright yellow, and I can't wear them out hunting like this," he said.

"Well, of course you can't," I replied. "Ask your new chap whether he used bleach when he washed them." This was exactly what had happened. Unfortunately, there was nothing that could be done to restore them.

Because bleach shortens the life of any cloth it shouldn't be used too frequently. Perhaps the simplest way of keeping white clothes white is to wear them often, because then you have them laundered frequently and they stay looking fresh. White garments that are not washable should go to the dry cleaner only occasionally, because the solvent used by dry cleaners isn't absolutely transparent and in time the garments pick up a gray tinge. Keep white clothes away from heat and light, which can turn them yellow.

HAND WASHING: Clothes that are labeled "Wash by hand" can be dry cleaned. But if, as I do, you wash them yourself, use a mild bar soap and a mild detergent. If you have sensitive skin, you should protect your hands by wearing rubber gloves. As you wash and rinse a washable woolen or delicate garment you must be careful not to wring or twist it; squeeze it to work the suds through the fabric. I rub soap directly onto the soiled areas of tougher fabrics and then rub the material together to create bubbles and loosen the dirt. Leave the garment immersed in water as you wash.

A single rinse is rarely enough to completely rid a garment of detergent. I ususally rinse three or four times before I am quite satisfied. I don't stop until the last rinsing water is absolutely clean, so clean you could drink it.

Never wring delicate garments and woolens. Gently squeeze the water out, spread the garment on a dry towel, roll the towel up like a sausage and squeeze again. And to avoid rust, I never place garments on metal hangers to dry. I always use wood or plastic.

MACHINE WASHING AND DRYING: Happily, the machines do the work. But there are a few tips worth remembering. Although I prefer to wash delicate articles by hand, this can be done by machine. You should, however, protect them from catching in the machine by putting them in a pillowcase before washing. To avoid creases, as soon as they have finished tumble drying remove them from the machine, shake them out and then hang or fold.

USING A DRY CLEANER: I suggest that you always go to a dry cleaner that does its work on the premises, rather than sending it to a central plant. There is less risk of clothes being lost, and in all likelihood you will receive better service.

Always empty the pockets before sending anything out. If your garment is stained, tell the cleaner what you think the stain is and when it occurred so he can gauge how much time it has had to set.

When you collect your clothes, see that everything was properly done. Make sure soil and stains are really gone, and if not, ask why. Check the pressing; there should be no creases in suit jacket sleeves. Trouser legs should have a single sharp crease, and all the little creases behind the knee should have completely disappeared.

TIE CARE: Silk ties cannot be washed or even dry cleaned without losing some of their color and shape. The most you can do for a soiled silk tie is to dry clean it and hope for the best. You can always hide it underneath a sweater. Knitted or tweed ties, however, can be hand washed with warm water and detergent, with one-third of a capful of ammonia added to two gallons of water for softening. To return the tie to its former shape, fold a large, fairly stiff envelope to the shape of the tie and push it up inside the broad end of the tie when the tie is half dry. The tie must be dried flat. When it is quite dry, remove the envelope.

CLEANING A BUTTON: A task most people don't face nowadays, but one that was very common when I was in service, was cleaning brass buttons. Our livery coattails were loaded with buttons that had to be cleaned daily; either you came up to standard in your general appearance or you were out. The problem was to clean the buttons without getting the polish on the fabric. We used a brass button stick for this. It was slit down the middle so the buttons could slide between the two sides and stay upright and steady. A cloth was placed underneath to keep the polish from falling on the coat. To polish a metal button, you can hold it away from the garment by inserting the prongs of a fork between button and fabric, or by putting a cloth round the crook of the button and holding it steady between your finger and thumb.

GREEN SOAP AND SODA: I am constantly amazed by how many different washing products there are on the market today. When I began in service, there were few choices. By and large we used plain soap when I was young—a mild soap on tweeds, woolens and delicate fabrics, and a green household soap, which we called scrubbing soap, on tougher fabrics. Green soap was bought by the hundredweight and came in wooden tubs about the size of a two-gallon barrel.

We used to scrub an awful lot of clothes. We kept the soap for a year, allowing the air to reach it so that it became thoroughly dried. It was as hard as brick when we came to use it, which made it last an especially long time; you could scrub with it right down to the end of the piece. Nowadays when you use a tablet of soap it becomes soft and mushy very quickly. I still use the old-style green soap for washing my hands, because I believe it is much more thorough than the scented soap that comes in tablets. I also use the green soap for scrubbing canvas bags.

Most of the soap tubs were kept for storing soda. Women used a few pinches of washing soda, a general cleansing agent, for laundering sheets and towels; these were not merely washed, but boiled. Soda was hard on the hands, and many people had bright red hands from using it. Most women's and workmen's hands appeared to be pickled; chapped and cracked hands were a real bugbear to us all. At night, most of us covered our hands with glycerin and mutton fat to keep them in good condition and then wore gloves to bed. Our hands were very much on display, and they had to look fresh.

In those days, a country house had its own laundry, consisting of at least one washing room, a drying room, and an ironing room. There might be a head laundry maid and two others to assist her with the general washing.

IRONING

All my life I have been looking after clothes and teaching others to do the same. Over the years I have found that many tried and true methods, which have been superseded by innovations of various kinds, still produce the best results. I have always been against gimmicks, and I consider the steam iron a bit of a gimmick, although I know that nearly everyone now has one, and they do work well. Clothes of course should be ironed while they are slightly damp, so I can appreciate the convenience of a steam iron. I still use a relatively old-fashioned iron. I just sprinkle my garments with water and roll them up in a towel or dampen them with a hand-pump spray mister, the type that is used to water plants. I don't feel that a steam iron would be more efficient, for by the time I've filled it with water I might as well have damped a cloth, which would have to be used to protect the fabric from the iron anyway.

During my days as footman and my early years as valet, most of us used solid, crudely shaped flatirons instead of an electric iron. This was because flatirons were heated on a stove, and this saved on electricity. Most houses generated their own power, and there was little to spare.

The flatirons went up to six or seven pounds in weight. The special billiard table iron weighed fourteen or fifteen pounds. The heavier the cloth, the heavier the iron I used. For pure wool evening clothes I used a medium-weight iron of up to five pounds, and if I was pressing a very fine suit I used a lighter iron, up to one and a half to two pounds. None of the houses let one go short; I usually had three or four irons of the same weight. Two of us could then work on similar clothes at the same time. And when my iron cooled, after about a quarter of an hour, I could exchange it for a hotter one off the stove.

We always gave a sleek finish to the silk top hats that were worn out hunting, and to hunting and city bowlers. We did this by ironing them with special hat irons. These were made of smooth metal and had beveled edges. There was one kind of iron for the side of the hat, which was approximately an inch and a half wide, and one for ironing underneath the curl of the brim, which was a narrow, curved iron with a long handle. We sometimes used a third iron for the crown; this was broader than, but similar in shape to, the one we used for the sides.

Because they were so small and fine, hat irons could be heated in an instant, unlike the flatirons, which had to be kept permanently on the stove to warm through. The hat irons were kept in the pantry, so we didn't have to go far if we needed to give a gentleman's hat a quick press. We could pop into the front hall and hand him his hat as he went out of the door.

TO IRON

The rules I learned in the beginning have held up. Never put an iron–any kind of iron–directly on men's suitings, most skirts and dresses, slacks, jeans, corduroys or wool sweaters. If you do, the fabric will probably come up shiny, and shine, as a rule, implies wear. Protect the surface with a cloth. Use a clean Irish linen tea towel or dish towel or a finished cotton cloth that won't leave any fluff behind. You should use a slightly damp cloth on top of all wool, tweed and corduroy suitings, but a dry cloth can be used on lightweight suitings such as linen and cotton. To damp the cloth, first wet it thoroughly and then wring it out very firmly, leaving it reasonably dry. The wringing is important, for if the cloth is too wet the steam can roll up and scald your hand, as well as make the clothes wet.

I always press lightweight fabrics before doing items made of heavier materials. This way I can allow the heat in the iron to mount. It seems a waste of time to have to wait for an iron to cool. You should always read the label in your garment to confirm how much heat it can take, and check the iron dial for heat instructions. A *hot* iron should never be used on manmade fibers, because heat will tend to melt the synthetic fabric. Drip-dry garments aren't supposed to need any ironing, but synthetics of course do need some pressing; it will given even permanent press garments a much better finish. However, never use more than a moderate heat.

Brush trousers or any garment that is made from heavy fabric with your clothes brush before pressing, then iron downwards, following the natural nap of the fabric. You don't need brute force; the weight of the iron does the pressing. Just keep the iron on the move so it doesn't leave its imprint through the damp cloth. If it happens that you do create an imprint, remove the cloth immediately and wait a few seconds. Then replace the cloth and carry on ironing. Nine times out of ten the mark will simply disappear.

To restore crushed or creased velvet, steaming is the answer. Hold the garment near an iron wrapped with a damp cloth or a conventional steam iron. Or you can hang it in the bathroom while you are having a hot bath or shower, or hang it near a boiling kettle. When preparing coronation robes for wearing, I always had the kettles boiling furiously and hung the robes nearby.

We used to get our pressing cloths from the housekeeper. Sometimes we were given an old piece of Holland cloth, which was a tough glazed linen that came from Holland. It had been used as the housemaids' hearth sheet, which they knelt on when laying fires. A few layers of Holland cloth made an ideal ironing pad, as would any smooth tough fabric that can stand any amount of pounding and banging.

As a footman, I never saw a day pass when I was not asked to press something. Someone might come into the brushing room and say he had a little crinkle at the back of the knee of his trousers, and I would press it out. As a valet, I pressed my employer's trousers each time I put them away. But I'll give you a tip; the more you press, the more you have to press.

Pressing is purely for appearance. It doesn't do anything for the good of the garment. On the contrary, even smoothing the cloth with the iron rubs it and creates wear. And although natural fibers like the effect of the steam—it opens them up and allows them to breathe—you are subjecting them to an extreme of temperature that they are not used to, and this can weaken them.

Thus, it is not wise to press the same garment too often. Nor is it a good idea to freshen up worn clothes too frequently by pressing; you're really just sealing in the wear marks.

IRONING BOARDS: One of the first ironing boards I remember seeing upon entering service was an actual board propped up between a table and a chair and covered with a blanket. Any flat wood surface can in fact be used as an ironing board. A sleeve board is handy for putting a finer finish on dress or shirt sleeves, and Barbara finds a commercial ironing board useful for turning her dresses and skirts. But I still prefer to iron my clothes on a table, which is all I feel I need. The wood must of course be covered. I lay a blanket down as a pad and cover it with a sheet. This gives a smooth surface and protects the garment from fluff.

IRON MAINTENANCE: Spray starch can give body and finish to lightweight fabrics, but be careful when using it. It can stick to the bottom of your iron and mark the next item you press. To avoid this kind of marking, unplug the iron after pressing a starched garment and allow it to cool. Then wipe the surface of the iron with a dry cloth, reheat the iron and resume your work.

If necessary, you can clean an iron easily by brushing it lightly with fine steel wool. A trick that I use is to wrap a candle or a piece of solid wax in a piece of heavy, tightly woven cloth, such as drill, and run the hot iron over it. This melts the wax into and through the cloth and gives a smooth finish to your iron, so it needs cleaning less often.

SUITS: Most don't need daily pressing; creases fall out after they have been hung in the cupboard. Some new jackets can go for months without being pressed. It depends, of course, on the person who is wearing the garment and how well it fits. Trousers need more frequent pressing because of the seat and the knee, which tend to bag from going upstairs and downstairs and from sitting. But if a man (or today, a woman) pulls the trouser legs up a few inches at the knee when sitting down, it saves the knee from becoming quite so baggy.

TROUSERS: The front leg crease is the most important part of the trousers to be ironed. It should be sharp and crisp. The front and back creases on each leg are midway between the two side seams. Pick the trousers up by the cuffs and line up the four seams. This will indicate the correct positioning of the creases.

Lay the trousers on the ironing surface so that the front crease is nearest to you. It doesn't matter whether the left or right leg is on top. The bottom pant leg should be ironed first; if you iron both legs together, the top leg will mark the bottom one. Fold the top leg back (as well as the material on both sides from the waistband to the crotch as in illustration 2) to iron the leg underneath. With the top leg folded back, smooth the bottom leg so it is ready for ironing. Lay a cloth over it. And be certain that your pressing cloth is smooth; if not, it will wrinkle the trouser leg.

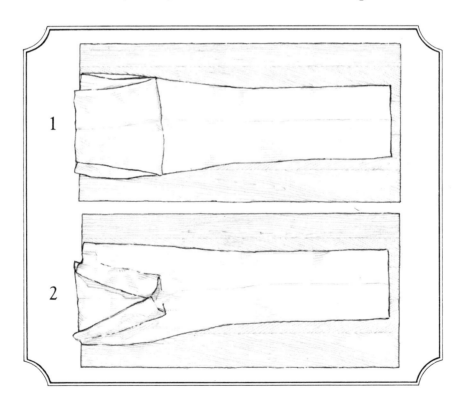

Begin by pressing the front crease. Bring the iron from the top of the pant leg to the cuffs. Repeat, always working downwards. Then iron the side of the leg, remembering to work downwards. There is no need to iron both sides of each leg, because the warmth and steam go straight through. You can see the steam marks underneath when you have finished.

After pressing the first leg, turn the trousers over so that the finished leg lies on top of the second, unpressed leg. Pull back the first leg and iron the second leg beneath it.

There are no special tricks for pressing the seat and front of the trousers. Just lightly press the natural contours, moving the iron downwards.

Perhaps the ideal way to care for pants, certainly the easiest, is to use a trouser press. It is just about foolproof to work; it gives off very gentle, steamy heat and keeps the trousers in perfect shape. I consider it a very good investment. I use a trouser press whenever I am staying in a hotel that has one; as soon as I undress I just pop my trousers in.

JACKETS: I iron my jackets as seldom as possible, because– as I mentioned–the more you press, the more you have to press. A jacket is specially "built" and should not crease from normal wear; the front remains relatively stiff, and the waist should keep its line. The only place where a jacket may need an occasional press is the inside of the elbows, which come under constant strain and will in time wrinkle with wear. Cover the wrinkled area with a very damp cloth before pressing. Be sure you do not press a crease into the jacket sleeve. The best thing to do with the rest of the jacket is to brush it, using a slightly damp brush. Brush it up against the nap and when you brush it down again the wrinkles will have disappeared. Steam, rather than press, a crumpled jacket lining. Turn your jacket inside out and hang it near a boiling kettle, or–perhaps easier these days–hang it in the vicinity of a steaming shower. The creases will vanish.

SKIRTS: Iron the lining first. Next, press the waistband. Then turn the skirt round the board, ironing from the waistband to the hem. Start at the back, because if something goes wrong it will be less noticeable. Avoid pressing the pockets, which may leave an outline on the outer fabric.

DRESSES: Begin by laying the back of the dress on the ironing board. Iron the collar, the yoke and the shoulders first. Then, turning the dress, iron the front and both sides, working from the collar to the hem. Give the front a second, final press. Touch up the collar with the iron to make it sit correctly. Press sleeves and cuffs last using a sleeve board. If the dress has ties at the back, iron them last of all.

JEANS: The ironing sequence is the same as for other trousers, except you do both sides of each leg. Press them with a damp cloth, or if they are still damp from washing, with a dry cloth.

SWEATERS: Use a warm, not hot, iron and a damp cloth. Pressing lightly, work down from the yoke to the waist. I always iron the back and front before doing the sleeves.

SHIRTS: I like to have shirts slightly damp. With cotton and most blends for daytime wear, there's no need to use a cloth under the iron. It is advisable, however, to use a damp cloth on inexpensive crepes and on satins so the iron marks don't show.

Iron the back first, starting with the yoke, the collar and the shoulders. Then lay the shirt front on the board. Iron round, rather than over, the buttons. Iron from top to bottom.

If you are ironing on a table rather than a commercial ironing board, button the middle button and iron the front in one piece. Then button the neck button, turn the collar down and press the points. The sleeves and cuffs should be worked on last.

TIES: There is no need to iron a knitted or tweed tie after you have washed it and allowed it to dry as described on page 62. But if a silk tie has become crumpled, I always steam rather than iron it so that it does not become shiny. I wrap the face of the iron with a damp cloth to generate steam. Then I hold the steaming cloth over the tie, close to it but not touching it directly.

AIRING CLOTHES

It is always wise to air clothes after ironing. Although they may feel dry because they are warm, they may still be slightly damp. Clothes must be bone dry before you wear them or you risk catching a chill. Also, if a garment is not completely dry when you put it on, the creases will fall out and it will lose its crisp appearance. You should allow your clothes to air for at least half an hour, although the longer you can leave them, the better.

Clothes should be aired in sunshine; in a warm cupboard where the temperature is above sixty degrees Fahrenheit; or in an airing cupboard which is specially made for airing and drying clothes. Most airing cupboards are built around hot pipes which give off their own natural heat. They are ventilated and fitted with clothes racks.

Clothes absorb the smell of tobacco and of trains, and also the fumes of the city where you live or work. When I opened certain visitors' cases (Sir Harold Nicolson's, for one) to unpack their things, I noticed their clothes had a stale London smell about them. On a hot day fresh air is ideal for airing any garment and for removing odors. A household spray with a mild fragrance also helps. After spraying the garment, give it a thorough brush both up and down the nap (see page 53). Then hang it by an open window for five or ten minutes until the smell of the spray has disappeared.

Hanging clothes in the bathroom while you're taking a bath or shower is another good way to eliminate smells. Shake the garment first. (Hold a skirt or pair of trousers by the waistband, and a jacket by the shoulders.) Afterwards hang it in the bathroom with the door closed to keep in the steam. When you have finished your ablutions, hang it by an open window in your bedroom. When the garment feels quite dry, return it to your wardrobe. To eliminate any moisture that might remain, leave the wardrobe doors open for at least fifteen minutes.

In the old days tobacco had a rich pungent smell, which, sadly, it doesn't have anymore. It was really fragrant, whether it was a pipe, cigar, or cigarette. When gentlemen lit up in the library after breakfast, the room smelled delicious. Oddly enough, velvet smoking jackets didn't absorb the smell as much as other clothes, unless the gentleman was a habitual cigar smoker. Lord Edward Gleichen was the heaviest cigar smoker I ever met. He smoked ten to twelve cigars every day, and his clothes reeked–but it certainly kept the moths at bay.

MENDING

A man can usually find someone to do his mending for him. Most men ask a wife or girl friend. But I think it is important for a man to look after himself. I do my own darning and sew on my own buttons whenever necessary. I have a handy pocket sewing kit, but for most basic mending all you need is a packet of needles–those with fairly large eyes are easiest to thread–and a selection of spools of thread in common colors. If you are not experienced at sewing, you should not undertake anything more complicated than sewing on a button, closing a ripped seam or simple darning.

TO SEW ON A BUTTON: You should use extra strong thread for sewing buttons on heavy garments such as jackets and coats, and it is essential for trouser buttons. On other items I double ordinary thread.

Poke the thread through the eye of the needle; it sometimes helps to lick the end first. When you have pulled it through and doubled the thread, knot the end with a loop knot. Position the button carefully and make sure the correct side of the button is showing.

Stitch from the very back of the material and through the holes in the button. Do not pull the stitches tight, but leave about an eighth of an inch of thread between the cloth and the button — more for heavy fabrics. Crisscross the thread at least six times on a four-hole button to make a firm X. Then wrap the thread three or four times round the shank (the thread between the cloth and the button) to really strengthen it. Finish off with two tiny stitches

through your stitches at the back. Make a knot and trim off the ends.
TO MEND A SEAM: Make a firm start with a stitch knot, or knot the thread before you begin. Begin sewing an inch above where the seam has come apart, follow the line of stitch marks and finish an inch below the end of the opening. Finish off with a knot.

STORING CLOTHES

Never leave clothes lying scattered about your room. It's just as easy to put them away as to drop them on the floor. Your clothes are more likely to stay in good condition if you put them away properly. It is easiest to do this and to find things again when you want them if your cupboard is orderly.

I like to keep my suits for each season together, clothes made from the same weight fabric together and all my evening clothes together. I have all my thicker trousers at one end of the cupboard and my very thin ones at the other end. If your cupboard doesn't look neat, your clothes will not look neat. I checked the third lord's clothes at least once a day. If he pulled something out and didn't put it back straight, I would rearrange it correctly as soon as I saw what had happened.

I do not like wire hangers and don't advocate using them. They aren't strong, they are likely to rust and they do leave a mark on fine materials. There used to be no such things. Dry cleaners returned clothes on wooden hangers with wire crooks, which we replaced with stainless steel ones to safeguard against rust. Wooden hangers are ideal; next best is plastic, as long as it can take the weight of your garment.

A three-piece suit should be on one hanger so parts of it won't become misplaced in your wardrobe. I hang my suits on double-barred wooden hangers. I fold my trousers over the lower bar and arrange my waistcoat and jacket on the top bar.

TROUSERS: Hang your trousers first. Keep them in the center of the hanger so they don't bunch up at one end and crease. Never hang trousers at the knee, as this area suffers the most wear. I hang my trousers approximately four to six inches above the knee.

WAISTCOATS: I always make sure that the crook of the hanger is centered and that my waistcoat is hanging straight and looks smooth. I keep it unbuttoned ready for wear.

JACKETS: Put a jacket on a hanger carefully so as not to ruffle the shoulders of the waistcoat underneath. The center of the collar must lie against the crook of the hanger so that the jacket hangs straight. There should be no bulges anywhere to spoil its line, so remove everything from the pockets. To save the sleeves from becoming crushed, put them a little in front of the jacket, so they are half over the pockets.

You'll find that if a jacket hasn't been worn for about a month, the shoulders become a bit dusty from the dust caused by the pulling out of your other clothes. If there is a lady using powder in the same room where your cupboard is, this too creates dust. I used to hang a sheet of tissue from the crook of every hanger so that half of it fell over the back of the jacket and the other half fell over the front. This covered the lapels and kept the shoulders free of dust. The waistcoat and trousers were protected inside the jacket.

DRESSES: Barbara makes sure that the crook of the hanger is at the center of the collar, so that her dress is correctly balanced on the hanger. Dresses should hang straight and look smooth. You should never let part of a sleeve stick out, or it will crease. Make sure the cuffs lie flat against the skirt. You can't make hard and fast rules as to where they should come on the skirt, as this depends on the length of the sleeves and the size of the woman.

COATS AND RAINCOATS: Hang a coat or raincoat on a single-barred hanger. Make sure the crook of the hanger is at the center of the collar, that there is nothing in the pockets and that the sleeves are hanging straight. Put them a little in front of your coat so they don't become crushed.

HOW STANLEY
AGER HANGS
GARMENTS

TIES: I prefer hanging most of my ties to folding them, and I have a tie rack on the back of my cupboard door. You must never drape your ties, one on top of the other, over a single hook. You could drape a towel over the crossbar of a hanger and hang your ties on that. Knit ties are better folded, because they can become stretched from hanging on a tie rack. I keep mine in my drawer.

Fold a tie in half at the neck, and then fold in half again. Lay each tie over the next so they fan out in your drawer, and you can see part of each tie.

SHOES: Do not pile your shoes one on top of the other, as the soles of the top shoes will scratch and dirty the shoes underneath. If you have only a few pairs, you can hook the heels over a shoe bar at the bottom of the closet. The best idea is to make a small shoe rack. Any small space will do. All you need for it are two rails, one to support the toes, and the other a little higher to catch the heels.

HATS: I have looked after a good number of hats in my time—hunting hats, cricket caps, shooting hats, opera hats, felt hats. A gentleman had at least seven different trilbies to match his various outfits. He would also have one bowler, one tall black hat for funerals and receptions at the palace, one tall gray hat for weddings and Ascot, as well as one opera hat, which was a tall hat that could be folded. I kept each set of hats together.

I always try not to put one hat inside the other. If I must, however, I make certain there is greaseproof paper inside the crown that will hold the second hat. I also wrap tissue paper round the outside crown of the second hat. This is a safety measure of mine to prevent the second hat from becoming smeared with hair lotion from inside the first hat.

FOLDING AND STORING

None of my footmen ever started out folding clothes quite the way I did. They folded a garment either a bit too much or too little so that it resembled a bundle rather than a flat package. But folding correctly is a knack that can be learnt, and they learnt in the end—most of them picked it up in two or three months.

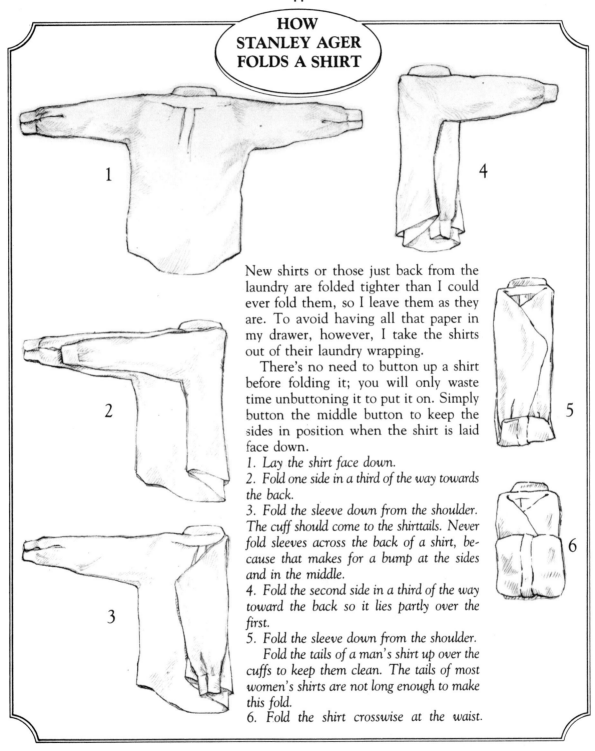

HOW STANLEY AGER FOLDS A SHIRT

New shirts or those just back from the laundry are folded tighter than I could ever fold them, so I leave them as they are. To avoid having all that paper in my drawer, however, I take the shirts out of their laundry wrapping.

There's no need to button up a shirt before folding it; you will only waste time unbuttoning it to put it on. Simply button the middle button to keep the sides in position when the shirt is laid face down.

1. *Lay the shirt face down.*
2. *Fold one side in a third of the way towards the back.*
3. *Fold the sleeve down from the shoulder. The cuff should come to the shirttails. Never fold sleeves across the back of a shirt, because that makes for a bump at the sides and in the middle.*
4. *Fold the second side in a third of the way toward the back so it lies partly over the first.*
5. *Fold the sleeve down from the shoulder.*

Fold the tails of a man's shirt up over the cuffs to keep them clean. The tails of most women's shirts are not long enough to make this fold.
6. *Fold the shirt crosswise at the waist.*

I never saw a gentleman wear a soft evening shirt until after the last war. Everyone used to wear dress shirts, which we called boiled shirts. The fronts were polished with special polishing irons by the laundry. I have no idea how this was done, but it is an old art and a laundry secret. This kind of shirt was buttoned with studs and was worn with a detachable wing collar. Today, dress shirts and wing collars are worn with a white tie and tails on very formal occasions. They should only be worn once before laundering. I keep mine in its laundry bag on its return. And although I dislike having too much paper in my drawer, I do the same with all evening shirts, which should also be laundered after a single wearing. I arrange them in a pile separate from the rest of my shirts to avoid handling them needlessly.

You should fold an evening shirt the same way you would fold an everyday shirt. The only difference is that you must lay it face down on tissue paper before you begin folding. I always use at least a couple of sheets of tissue, because one sheet is too thin and may tear. After folding the shirt at the waist, use the rest of the tissue to cover the back, then turn the shirt over and tuck under the ends of the tissue to make a tidy parcel before putting it away.

SHIRT STORAGE: I like to be certain which shirt I am going to wear before I take it out of the drawer. If you choose one shirt and then change your mind and exchange it for another, in time your drawer is going to look an awful muddle. I store my shirts so that as much as possible of each can be seen. Depending on the size of the drawer, I can see half, a quarter or just the edge of each of my shirts. Best of all is to lay them out in a terraced manner from bottom back towards the top so you can remove one without dislodging the others. But if your drawers aren't large enough, you can create a graduated stack–one over the other–so there is always some color showing, and you know which is which.

I place shirts in a drawer so the collars face away from me and the front edges face towards me. I do this because I prefer to avoid handling collars, which are always on show. The edge of a folded shirt is at the waist, which is not on public view, so handling is less likely to affect the shirt's appearance when worn.

If your storage space is small, there may not be room to slip a shirt out from under the rest without disturbing your arrangement. If this is the case, you must lift up all your shirts that are on top of the one you want, carefully remove it and then put the rest back as they were. Never try to pull one out from under the others. You cannot hope to put them back into place afterwards. You will untidy the rest of your shirts and have a messy-looking shelf or drawer.

If you are going to wear a shirt again before having it washed, fold it and put it on top of your clean ones because you should wear it soon. I would never keep a worn shirt in a drawer for longer than two consecutive days.

SWEATER STORAGE: A woman will wear a sweater and then change into another the following day, whereas a man may wear the same one for days on end. Invariably he has favorite clothes. He'll wear the same garment constantly, and then suddenly he will take another favorite and wear that. This is when the first one needs to be washed.

My sweaters are folded the same way as my shirts. I keep my clean sweaters in a separate pile. Barbara wraps her fine sweaters in tissue paper and folds them in tissue paper as though she was folding an evening shirt. She keeps them separate from all the other sweaters in her drawer.

A fine soft sweater, such as a cashmere or angora sweater, must be folded carefully. Place tissue paper between the folds to avoid knife-edge creases. Cover it with tissue for additional protection, and–in the case of angora–to prevent shedding.

Lay the sweater face down on tissue paper. Fold the sleeves across the back to minimize the number of folds. Cover with a second piece of tissue. Fold the sweater crosswise at the waist. Cover with the ends of the tissue paper, or if there is not enough, use a third sheet.

STORAGE PRECAUTIONS

You don't need to take elaborate precautions with clothes that are in constant use because you can look after them as you wear them. Garments that are not frequently worn should be checked once a week for general condition. You should make this a matter of routine, and not something to do just when you think about it—regularity is the essence of clothes care.

MOTH PROTECTION: As you regularly flip through your clothes, you will flush out any moths that might be settling in your cupboard. Fine wool evening clothes are beloved by moths, and should always be kept separately so you can quickly run your fingers through them to keep the moths at bay. I kept my employer's morning coat—this was made of the purest wool—with his evening clothes. Moths prefer tweed after fine wool, but they will always settle for woolen underwear and sweaters. Everything else—cotton, linen and manmade fibers—is safe, as these fibers do not provide the sustenance that moths require. Actually, it's not the moth that eats wool, but the grub that hatches from the moth's egg, a barely visible caterpillar. The moth lays its eggs in sheltered areas such as trouser cuffs or under the sleeves of jackets.

Some people use mothballs or aerosol moth repellent sprays to protect their clothes. The real drawback to mothballs is that unless your clothes have been out in the air for about twelve hours they will hold the smell. What self-respecting gentleman goes out smelling of mothballs? In the old days they used a variety of herbs in pomanders to keep moths away. Today you can use potpourri, which is just as effective as camphor but has an attractive scent. A less expensive deterrent is a small bunch of five or six bay leaves tied together and hung in your cupboard. Use a needle to thread a piece of cotton through the bottom of the leaves near the stem. Then tie the ends round your wardrobe rail. Leave the cotton long enough for the leaves to come below the crooks of the hangers. Keep them fresh and really fragrant by changing them every three or four months.

Bay leaves or potpourri will also protect your clothes against silverfish, small pests about a quarter of an inch long. They are quite harmless but a nuisance to have running around in your clothes.

CLIMATE: Most things should be stored in a dry place at an even temperature, and clothes are no exception. If a garment is kept in a humid atmosphere or exposed to excessive damp and then allowed to dry out slowly, mildew will result. If your cupboard is damp, remove your clothes immediately and find out where the moisture is coming from.

LONG-TERM STORAGE: I put my clothes in light plastic clothes bags if I won't be wearing them for a couple of months, to save checking them. Use either a plastic clothes bag with a zipper at the side or the plastic bags dry cleaning is returned in. These must be tied very firmly at the bottom so that tiny moths cannot enter and mother moths cannot lay eggs down a crack.

Clothes should be thoroughly cleaned before they are put away. And when I say cleaned, I mean really cleaned–dry cleaned, or completely brushed and pressed with a hot iron, as hot as is safe for the fabric. If clothes are to be stored on wire hangers, make sure there is some kind of protective covering on the hangers to lessen the risk of rust.

At the start of the summer we always cleared our employer's wardrobe of heavy winter clothes to make room for the summer clothes. The winter ones were cleaned and packed away until the following October. I would never put clothes in a plastic bag if they were to be stored for longer than three or four months. They are much safer locked in a trunk.

Barbara and I need three trunks to hold all our different garments. We pack everything according to its weight: the heavier garments are packed first, with the lighter garments on top. In one trunk I pack winter clothes and country clothes, my tweed jackets, wool trousers and corduroy trousers. I put my summer clothes in a second trunk, as well as my evening clothes and smarter suits. A pin-stripe suit, for instance, would go in here. Barbara packs her better dresses and skirts and her evening clothes in this trunk.

The last trunk is the linen trunk. This is where I put all the shirts and underwear. And I also put my sweaters and socks in here.

I pack sachets of potpourri between the layers as a protection against moths and cover the last layer of clothes with tissue paper. Then I seal each trunk with tape to protect the contents from dust.

If I was storing clothes in a trunk at home, I would check them every six months to be certain there are no moths and that some freshness is being maintained. I always shake clothes when checking them and, if possible, brush them out.

I packed away all my working clothes when I went off to the army, and I didn't unpack them again until I returned, five and a quarter years later. Then I opened my trunk, put on my tailcoat and went straightaway that morning to wait at lunch. Not a crease!

SHOE AND LEATHER CARE

If your shoes are not clean, you will not look well dressed no matter how smart your clothes are. I've always been very particular about shoes. I clean all my shoes before I wear them. Whenever I visited my sister I would say, "Now where are all your shoes?" Her family would make a great heap of their shoes and I would spend a couple of hours cleaning them. I get terrific satisfaction from a well-polished shoe, but a good shine is something that not everyone is able to achieve. Most people scrub at a shoe, when in fact, for a good deep shine, there should be a light quickness about the whole movement.

In the old days the look of a gentleman's shoes indicated the proficiency of his servant. A valet judged another valet's work by the look of his employer's boots and coat. But I remember one valet being quite upset after hearing someone say to his boss, "Your man can really clean shoes." To his way of thinking, any valet or footman presumably was able to clean shoes; he wished that person had remarked instead, "You have a good crease in your trousers."

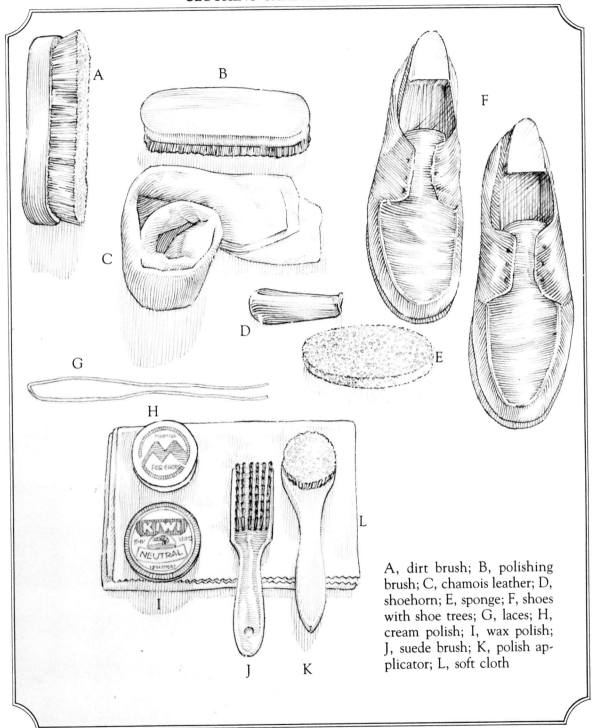

A, dirt brush; B, polishing brush; C, chamois leather; D, shoehorn; E, sponge; F, shoes with shoe trees; G, laces; H, cream polish; I, wax polish; J, suede brush; K, polish applicator; L, soft cloth

We cleaned all our boots and shoes in the boot hall. We called it the boot 'ole, because although it was kept tidy and it was light enough, it always seemed dirty from the mud off the shoes and the blacking we used. If you worked for hunting people, the room needed to measure at least twelve feet by six to give you elbow room for cleaning their boots. You had to have a good strong table to work on and a deep sink for scrubbing boots, with a rack nearby where they could be turned upside down to drain.

Each footman had his own drawer where he kept his cleaning things, while the valet kept his things locked in his shoebox in his own corner, quite separate from everyone else's. Unless the valet was a particular friend of one of the footmen or he thought one of them showed promise, no footman would come in while the valet was cleaning his shoes. Footmen knew there were certain things a valet kept to himself, such as small tricks that made his shoe cleaning different from anyone else's. Not everyone knew to clean the instep of a shoe, or to clean between the stitches on the instep, and they weren't familiar with lifting the flaps on lace-ups to clean underneath them, or with cleaning the tongue.

A valet's most important secret involved the varnishers and the particular type of vinegar that he added to the blacking. Wine vinegar was best, but to obtain this a valet had to be on good terms with the cook, who supplied it out of her kitchen. This was not something that a footman could easily ask for, but the valet had a good opportunity when he sat down with the cook for meals in the housekeeper's room. And he had the added advantage of being able to bring her back a present when he returned from a trip abroad with his employer.

One of the real problems of my work was sore feet. It was not simply because we were always on our feet but because we continually walked across different kinds of floors. We might go from stone onto very soft rugs and perhaps back onto cold slate after our feet had become hot from running on carpet.

Many of the people I worked with developed flat feet. One of the things I blamed this on was having a board in front of the sink where, as footmen, we stood to wash up. This meant we had to stand with our ankles twisted and our feet turned out at a quarter to three for hours on end. Whether this actually caused flat feet I don't know. But as a butler I always arranged things so that my footmen could have their feet straight under the sink.

SHOEHORNS

I always have a shoehorn. The one I carry with me is tin, and I have had it for fifty years. I never put a shoe on without one. There is no other way to avoid pressing down the back of a shoe. If you don't own a shoehorn, use the back of a spoon handle.

Every morning when I laid out the second lord's clothes, I would put his shoes by the chair where he sat to put them on and his shoehorn on top of them. All he had to do was reach down, pick up the shoehorn, slide it into each shoe and then put it on. One day the bell rang just after I left him, and I wondered what on earth he wanted. "Where's my shoehorn?" he demanded, when I went back to his room. It was next to him on the dressing table, closer than the bell he used for summoning me. "It shouldn't be there, it should be here," he said, pointing to its usual place by his shoes.

SHOE TREES

Always put shoe trees into your shoes as soon as you take the shoes off. This is essential. After your shoes have taken the weight of your body throughout the day, they have stretched out of shape. By putting trees in while the shoes are still warm from the wearing, and therefore malleable, you can bring them back into shape. This is particularly important for people who have kinks in their shoes because of the way they walk. Never put a tree in a cold shoe; it will crack the leather and stretch the shoe in the wrong places.

The tree must fit the shoe. If it is too big, it will stretch the leather and can pull the stitches on a sewn shoe. If it is too small, it will fail to offer proper support.

I have a pair of wooden shoe trees shaped like feet. They are over a hundred years old and were given to me by a valet before I went to work at Dunsany. The best trees, I feel, are rigid ones made of wood or metal. Wooden and fabric-covered shoe trees help dispel the moisture that accumulates inside the shoe. Wood absorbs the moisture, and fabric allows air to circulate. Wooden shoe trees also allow leather to breathe after it has become wet. A pair of damp shoes should never be left without some inside support; however, it is best to stuff them with newspaper until they have dried before inserting the trees. If you don't own a pair of trees, at least stuff a pair of rolled-up socks into the toe part of the shoe, which needs more support than the heel.

I tree both the foot and the leg of a lady's boot. Either buy trees for the legs or make cylinders for them out of cardboard. Trees for boot legs should not stretch the leather, but should push it out only far enough so that it appears smooth.

In order not to stretch lace-up shoes, always undo the laces before you take them off. Notice when the heels of your shoes become too thin; this not only looks unattractive, it can ruin the shape of the shoe by shifting the way your foot settles into it. Never leave boots or shoes near heat, as this will crack the leather. And always keep patent leather shoes wrapped for extra protection.

WASHING SHOES

I wash my shoes once a month to rid them of stale perspiration and to remove the dust caught in the seams, which on sewn shoes will cut the stitches.

All hard-wearing leather shoes can be immersed in water. These include moccasins, gym shoes, men's lace-ups and casual shoes and ladies' tough leather shoes. Only shoes with leather heels should be submerged; these are recognizable by thin leather bands running around the heels. I am wary of washing shoes that have a smooth leather finish, as they could wrinkle when thoroughly wetted; I give them the same careful treatment as fine leather shoes.

EQUIPMENT: I wash my shoes with a sponge or a soft nailbrush. A coarse bristle dirt brush is ideal for brushing or scrubbing mud off strong leather shoes, such as shooting or fishing shoes, but will scratch finer, soft leathers.

WATER: I use cold or lukewarm water with a drop of ammonia added for a softening effect. (The amount of ammonia should not even be enough to cover the bottom of the bottle cap.) Better still is to wash shoes in cooled boiled water, in a sink. If I was caught by the tide when walking from the mainland to the Mount, I immersed and rinsed my shoes in fresh water as soon as I arrived to rid them of the salt. In fact I submerged them in a tub of rainwater.

Wash shoes thoroughly. You will not need to change the water unless your shoes are very muddy, or have been in contact with salt, in which case you will probably have to wash them twice. Then stand them upside down for a few minutes to allow the water to drain. Mop up any water that is left inside with an old cloth, and then pack them tightly with newspaper. Always pack wet shoes with newspaper immediately after they have drained, because this helps them keep their natural shape and absorbs the moisture.

DRYING: Shoes take at least twenty-four hours to dry. Let them dry naturally, preferably in the open air. Never dry them near heat. Repack them with fresh paper after twelve hours. And after another twelve hours your shoes should be almost dry. Even if they are still damp, you can discard the paper to allow air to circulate inside them. When they are nearly dry, tree them and rub a little cream into the leather to condition it. Later, when they are completely dry, rub the surface with a cloth to remove any cream that has not been absorbed. This will bring up a dullish shine. To shine them you must start again with a fresh smear of polish.

FINE LEATHER: Fine leather shoes, which include most ladies' shoes, should be treated with utmost care. They should not be immersed in water because the weight of the water could pull them out of shape. Instead, remove grit from between the sole and the upper by passing the instep under cold running water. Then sponge the inside clean; dip a sponge or soft nailbrush in a bowl of lukewarm water with a drop of ammonia added and wipe round the inside of the shoe. Pack the shoes with newspaper and let them dry naturally. When they are dry, tree them and polish them in the ordinary way. The inside of patent leather shoes, ladies' fragile shoes, evening shoes and sandals should only be dusted, not sponged, as water may harm them.

I am not afraid of washing suede shoes because I know the pitfalls, and I have the patience to wait three or four days for them to dry. If you do not, I suggest using suede shampoo and following the directions on the bottle.

POLISHING SHOES

It takes under four minutes to polish a pair of shoes—one minute to put on the polish, one minute to work it in, one minute to polish and half a minute or so to rub with the chamois.

EQUIPMENT: To polish shoes you need two brushes, a soft rag for applying polish and a genuine oil-dressed animal skin (not simulated) chamois leather. The first brush (which I refer to as the putter-onner) works the polish into the shoe; this prevents the buildup of excess polish which would cling to the bristles of your second brush, the polishing brush. The polishing brush brings up a shine. The chamois leather adds a much deeper shine and removes any remaining polish that could rub onto trouser cuffs or stockings.

POLISH: Shoe cream is usually sold in jars; wax polish is solid and comes in cans. Both are colored to match different shades of leather. Shoe cream preserves leather and keeps it supple, and wax polish creates a protective film and is water-resistant, so you should use cream and wax polish alternately. Kiwi wax and Meltonian cream are both excellent polishes. Saddle soap cleans leather but does not leave a shine like shoe cream or wax polish. Wax polish should be used to cover scratches.

Remove marks caused by accumulated polish with a transparent wax such as Kiwi Light Tan. Rub it very hard into the spot with a corner of a duster wrapped round your forefinger. If, after you have removed the spot, the color of the leather is lighter, rub the area again with a wax polish that is a shade darker than your shoe. A second cleaning will also add to the shine.

BRUSHES: In the old days we used three brushes on shoes—one hard, one less hard and the other a soft bristle. The first type, the dirt brush, is available today and so is the second which we used for putting on polish. But this type of brush is now also sold as a polishing brush, whereas I always polished with a long fine bristle brush. I have had mine for over fifty years and it is still in mint condition.

Nowadays you can apply polish with either a small circular brush that has a long handle or with a second "polishing" brush. Both are adequate, but if you use a polishing brush as a putter-onner, you should mark it as such to avoid confusion. In time, the bristles will become shorter and harder with wear, while the bristles of the polisher will stay the same length, since polishing is done with a lighter stroke.

CLEANING THE BRUSHES: Neither the polishing brush nor the putter-onner should ever be washed or allowed to become wet, which would make the bristles turn soft and mushy. They should need only occasional cleaning because there should never be too much polish on them in the first place. I clean brushes by brushing them on brown paper. I wrap a double layer of brown paper (dull side up) round the edge of a table. This makes a sharp enough surface to separate the bristles as the brush is rubbed up and down on the paper.

The dirt brush is constantly immersed in water. I simply rinse it under cold water when I have finished with it, then flick the water out of the bristles and let it dry naturally.

CHAMOIS LEATHERS: I have had my chamois since I was a boy, and it is as soft today as it was then. The art of caring for a chamois lies in the washing. I have always believed in washing everything in filtered rainwater, but this is a luxury that most people don't have these days. Instead, I fill a bowl with warm water–never hot, as chamois doesn't like the heat–and add ammonia (just enough to cover the bottom of the bottle cap) as a softener.

Rather than use detergent, I put a bar of household soap in with the chamois. Then I allow it to soak. I gently squeeze–never wring–the dirt out. When the water becomes dirty, I change it and carry on squeezing the chamois until all the dirt comes out and it is almost as clean as when I bought it.

Then I rinse it, and carry on rinsing until I see the water is absolutely clean, which entails changing it a couple of times. I take the chamois out of the water and put a light film of soap on the rough side–which is the side that is not used. I squeeze the leather until it feels nice and soft. I am lucky in being able to hang it outside on a line to dry. As it dries, rub the sides together to remove the soap.

TO POLISH SHOES: I always polish my shoes on a table with their shoe trees in them, holding them steady with my left hand. If you don't have shoe trees, put your hand inside each shoe to hold it in position.

There should be no dirt or dust on the shoe when you begin. Apply cream polish with a soft rag, because it would fall between the bristles of a brush. Put on only a smear at first; you can always add more, and too much cream polish can stick in the seams and mark a shoe. Work the polish in with your putter-onner. Use the putter-onner to apply wax polish; drag it across the tin, scraping off on the edge of the tin any lumps that may have accumulated on the bristles. Brush round and cover the shoe. Let the polish sit on the first shoe while you work polish into the second. This allows it to slowly soak into the leather so it won't be absorbed by your polishing brush.

The grain on leather is not visible and there is no rule governing the direction in which it should be polished. Generally a right-handed person polishes clockwise and a left-handed person anti-clockwise. No two people polish shoes or boots in the same manner–

either in the same direction or with the same amount of pressure. The one universal rule is that you should never scrub at a shoe when you polish it, as this will only ruin your brush and lessen the shine. With your polishing brush, brush round the shoe–again including the instep–with light strokes. Then make a pad out of your chamois and rub it over the shoe to heighten the shine.

PATENT LEATHER SHOES: We used cream polish on men's patent leather evening shoes, but Vaseline can also be used. Whichever you choose, apply it with a soft cloth. Use a clean part of the cloth for polishing. Newer patent leathers have a special coating that can be cleaned by wiping with a damp cloth.

SUEDE SHOES: These need brushing with a special suede brush to loosen surface dirt and raise the nap. Brush up the nap, and then brush down the nap, which is clockwise. You must brush the whole shoe in the same direction for a smooth finish.

LACE-UP SHOES: There is a knack to cleaning lace-up shoes. First of all you should remove the laces to prevent polish from falling on them and destroying their color. Then put a little polish on your putter-onner, turn back the flaps and rub polish into them. Hold them up with your left hand. Take your polishing brush in your right hand and shine the flaps with a few short brisk strokes. Then polish the rest of the shoe in the same way.

The tongue becomes dusty rather than dirty, but it should be cleaned for a proper finish. Slip your fingers underneath it so that it lies flat. Rub on a smear of polish with a brush, or–if it's easier–with a duster wrapped round your forefinger. Polish the tongue with a polishing brush or a clean part of the duster until it shines, and then finish the rest of the shoe.

BONING: We used to bone shoes and boots with blacking, a preparation that came in stone jars. The blacking was applied with a stick and the shoe was rubbed with a piece of bone. The friction of the bone against the leather pressed out the scratches and created a new surface as well as a tremendous polish. No one does that nowadays, as the leathers today wouldn't stand up to it; shoes had to be made of thick leather if they were to be boned.

I remember taking hold of the bone in both hands and resting my chin on top of the boot to steady it. Then I'd really work away. When I had finished boning, I brushed the surface with light strokes and watched the shine come up and come up. For a truly wonderful shine, I applied a little more polish and carried on brushing until it was absolutely brilliant. Finally I used a chamois on the boot so no marks would come off onto the wearer's trouser cuffs.

The best bone was from the foreleg of a deer, preferably a female deer, although some people maintained you could use the foreleg of a sheep. I still have one of my bones, which came from the foreleg of a female deer. It's about eight or nine inches long and about an inch wide, and the color is so brilliant you would think it was made of amber. We used to pick up bones when we went stalking in Scotland–there was always venison for dinner!

TRAVELING

Instead of traveling with shoe brushes, which add bulk to your packing, I recommend taking a couple of dusters for putting on either black or brown polish and a folded chamois for polishing.

Pack a pair of shoe trees and a shoehorn. Take a spare pair of laces for lace-up shoes; it is surprising how hard they can be to find. If you are traveling to a hot climate take shoe cream rather than wax polish, which melts easily.

Every valet had a heavy wooden shoe box holding all his shoe-cleaning materials, and I used to take mine with me when traveling. Finding porters was never a problem–they would fight to get your custom then. When the lady's maid and I traveled together, I cleaned her lady's shoes. Otherwise our work was quite distinct. On some occasions the lady's maid could be a bit of a nuisance; "You've got polish on my lady's laces" was one of her favorite complaints. At home she always cleaned the shoes herself, unless she could persuade the hallboy to do them for her, in which case she paid him. He was always out to earn a bob or two extra. When

I was a hallboy, I cleaned the chef's shoes for half a crown a week, which was half my wages again. But no sooner had I brought up a handsome polish on his shoes than he would wear them and drop fat on them! Only the top houses had chefs. They were mostly French, spoke broken English, had beastly tempers—and to cap it all were extremely fond of garlic, which I loathe!

LEATHER SUITCASES

I would use a well wrung out soapy cloth to sponge dirt off a suitcase, and wipe it with a dry cloth before rubbing a small amount of cream polish into the leather to condition it.

You must polish a heavy brown suitcase with a matching polish. You can use polishing brushes if the surface is large enough; otherwise work the polish in with a duster and shine with a soft cloth. Stand the case up and work round it, or polish both sides and then the two ends. I always finish off with a chamois leather to remove surface polish and give a deeper shine.

LEATHER BAGS AND BRIEFCASES

I am not keen on polishing a bag that will be held under your arm, because the heat of your body will make your clothes absorb the polish. I would recommend only wiping off fingermarks wth a well wrung out soapy cloth. Or you can apply a smear of colorless wax polish, which will not mark your clothes.

CANVAS BAGS

Clean canvas luggage by scrubbing, taking care not to wet any leather trim. You should dip a nailbrush in lukewarm water and detergent, then rub a little household soap on the bristles. Scrub round the bag until it appears clean. Then rinse off the soap with a damp cloth and let the canvas dry naturally.

Condition any leather trim with cream or a transparent wax polish.

PACKING WELL

When you take clothes out of your wardrobe, they should be ready for wear, ready for packing. If you brushed them before you put them away and kept them in a good tight wardrobe, they shouldn't want brushing before being put into the case. But do brush them when you unpack them. This helps get rid of any light creases and freshens them up.

TISSUE PAPER

It is impossible to pack properly without an ample supply of tissue paper. Used correctly, tissue paper protects garments and helps prevent wrinkling.

There are two kinds of tissue paper, acid and nonacid. Acid tissue paper is ordinary tissue, sometimes used for wrapping a loaf of bread. It is soft, tears easily and looks slightly yellow. Nonacid tissue is pure white. I use the toughest, whitest, thickest nonacid tissue paper I can find, which is the most practical for packing clothes. Women's clothes should be packed with more tissue paper than men's because they are generally made of softer material. A garment of particularly fine material, such as a silk dress, should be laid flat on tissue paper before folding.

FOLDING

For convenience, fold clothes on a bed or bedside table. I suggest you fold everything that requires folding before loading anything in the case.

HOW STANLEY AGER FOLDS TROUSERS

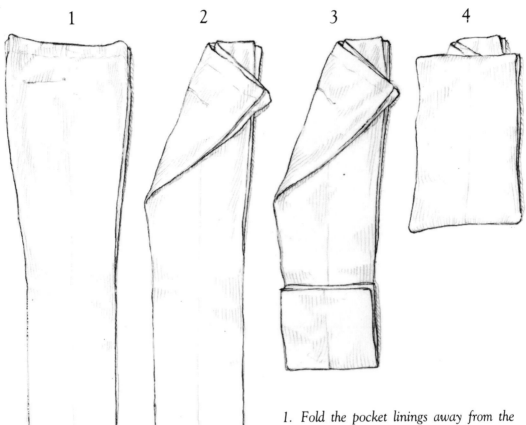

1   2   3   4

When you take trousers off the hanger to pack, they are already folded at the base of the seat. Make sure all the pockets are empty. Lay them flat.

1. Fold the pocket linings away from the front of the trouser legs so as not to interfere with the crease.
2. Fold the back of the waistband down and towards the front at an angle, as shown.
3. Fold up the trouser legs six inches or less below the knee. Avoid folding on the knee, which gets an enormous amount of wear.
4. Fold up again so the first fold reaches the waist.

HOW STANLEY AGER FOLDS A WAISTCOAT

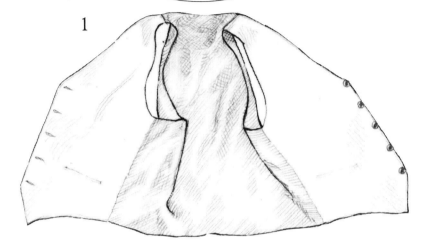

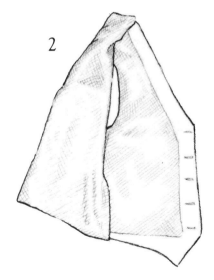

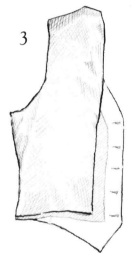

1. Lay the waistcoat flat, right side up, with the front panels showing.
2. Fold it lengthwise on the back seam, preserving the natural fold under the armhole. The two lower points will overlap.

3. Fold along the side seam beneath the armhole.
4. Fold the waistcoat in half crosswise, so that the narrow upper half is lying on the broad body of the waistcoat.

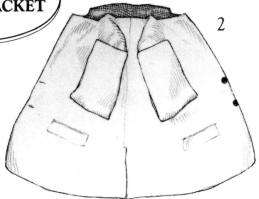

The way I pack a jacket, it should stay uncreased for at least three months. When we went out to East Africa by slow ship, we left England wearing winter clothes, and in the eastern Mediterranean we put them away for the rest of our trip. They weren't crumpled when we unpacked them a few months later on our return home.

Most people fold a jacket incorrectly. They fold the sleeves across the chest and, ignoring the waistline, fold the jacket from top to bottom. Then they squash it into the case, causing creases and making for bulky packing. A tailor folds a jacket better than most people; he puts it in a box specially made to fit his clothes and packs it with masses of tissue paper. But it is not necessary to put paper in the folds of a jacket, unless it is velvet or made of very soft fabric, if you pack it properly–preserving the natural folds at the waistline and seams.

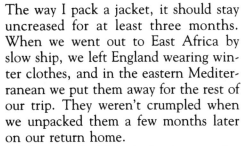

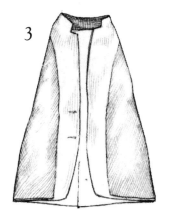 

1. Make sure the pockets are empty. Lay the jacket flat, lining side down. Turn the collar up so it lies flat; it is reinforced, so it will not crease.

2. Fold up both sleeves at the elbow so they are lying flat.

3. Fold back the sides of the jacket so that the front edges almost meet at the center back seam.

4. Fold the jacket on the center back seam, bringing the lapels together. The jacket is now long and thin, and there is a natural fold under each armhole.

Fold up at the waist. For neatness, tuck in any extra material from the coattails between the folds of the jacket.

HOW STANLEY AGER FOLDS AN EVENING SHIRT

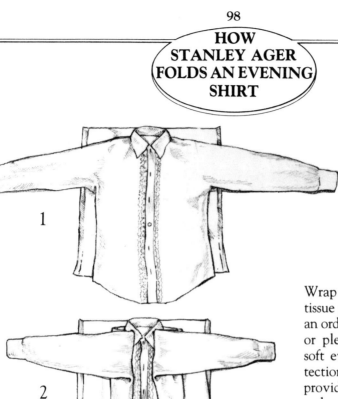

Wrap a soft silk evening shirt in tissue paper and fold it as you would an ordinary shirt (see page 77). Frills or pleats on a man's or woman's soft evening shirt need extra protection for packing. The best way to provide this is to cover the front, rather than the back, with the shirttails. Protect the front of a man's dress shirt by folding it the same way.

1. Begin by laying the shirt flat on its back on a piece of tissue paper. Button only the middle button.

2. Fold each side in a third of the way towards the front. The sides should just edge under the frills or pleats, to support them without crumpling them.

3. Fold down the sleeves to lie on their corresponding sides. The cuffs should come to the shirttails.

4. On a man's shirt, fold the tails up over the cuffs to keep them clean.

5. Fold the shirt crosswise at the waist.

Put a second piece of tissue paper over the shirt. Tuck under the ends to make a tidy parcel.

HOW STANLEY AGER FOLDS A SKIRT

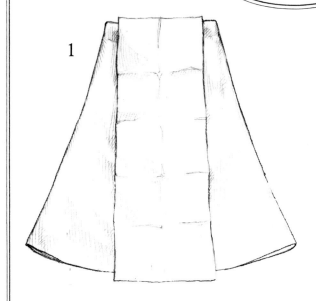

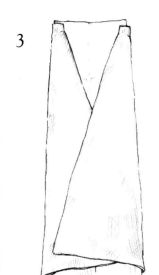

A flared or straight skirt should be folded into a rectangular shape to line up with the rest of the packing. Use tissue paper to prevent creasing.

1. Lay the skirt flat, face down. Lay a sheet of tissue paper in the center of the skirt; it should reach at least from the hem to the waistband.
2. Fold in one side of the skirt to make a straight line from the hem to the waistband.
3. Do the same with the opposite side.
4. Fold the skirt in half crosswise to make a rectangular package.

The best way to pack an accordion-pleated skirt is to put it inside a stocking. Lay each pleat on top of the next so the skirt forms a tight cylinder, then slip a stocking over the skirt to protect the pleats.

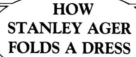

HOW STANLEY AGER FOLDS A DRESS

1

2

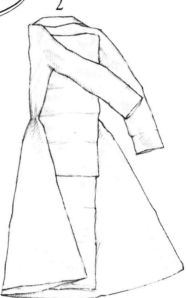

3

4

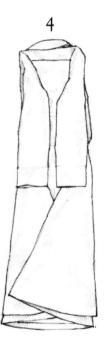

The upper half of a dress is folded like a shirt and the lower half is folded like a skirt, then the dress is folded in half at the waist. The object is to make a tidy parcel of the dress.

1. Lay the dress face down on your packing surface; make sure that it is lying flat. Put tissue paper in the center of the dress to guard against creasing.

2. Fold one side in a third of the way toward the back. The flare of the skirt should be folded in so that the outside edge becomes a straight line.

3. Fold back the sleeve so that it falls from the shoulder to the waist.

4. Repeat folds on the opposite side; lay the second folded flare on top of the first flare and fold back the sleeve.

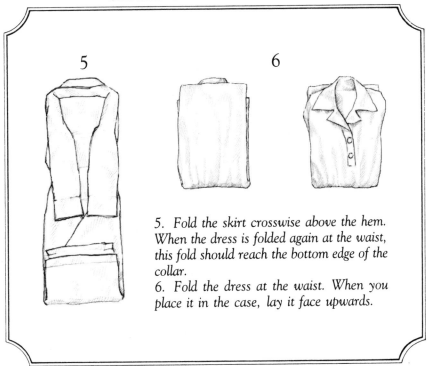

5. *Fold the skirt crosswise above the hem. When the dress is folded again at the waist, this fold should reach the bottom edge of the collar.*

6. *Fold the dress at the waist. When you place it in the case, lay it face upwards.*

SILK DRESS: A dress made of silk or any fine material is folded exactly the same way as an ordinary dress except that more tissue paper is required. Stuff both sleeves with tissue paper. Lay the dress face down on tissue paper so that the collar and front are protected, and cover the back with a sheet of tissue paper. Now fold the dress as you would an ordinary dress. Lay a sheet of tissue paper across the back so the dress is wrapped in a parcel of tissue. Lay it face upwards in the case.

LONG DRESS: Fold a long dress into a rectangle as you would a short dress. Never make it shorter than you need; the last fold should come at the waist. Pack it with lashings of tissue paper as you would a silk dress. Because of the length, use two sheets of tissue to cover the front when you first lay it flat, and more tissue to cover the back before you begin to shape your rectangle. At the finish it should be wrapped in a parcel of tissue.

SHIRT: A new shirt or a shirt that has just come back from the laundry should be kept in its bag. Do not pack shirts in airtight plastic containers, such as plastic bags used for storing food, because moisture may condense inside. (To fold a shirt for packing, see page 77.)

SWEATER: Lay the sweater face down. Fold the sleeves straight across the back or as you would fold shirt sleeves, from the shoulder to the bottom of the sweater. If you fold the sleeves down to the bottom, fold the sweater into a rectangle. Follow the steps for folding a woman's shirt, as there is no need to cover the cuffs. The sweater can be folded in half again, below the armhole, and tucked into a corner of your case. (To fold a sweater, see page 79.)

DRESSING GOWN: Fold a dressing gown into a large rectangle that can be spread over the rest of your packing to keep it tight. Turn it inside out and fold it at the waist.

RAINCOAT OR MACKINTOSH: Never roll up a raincoat for packing; this makes for creases in the raincoat, and the bulky shape can make creases in your other clothes.

Fold a raincoat exactly the same way as a jacket. Because of its length, fold tails up to the waist before folding the raincoat at the waist.

BELTS: Remove belts from garments and pack them separately. All belts should be rolled, rather than folded, to avoid sharp creases.

LINEN, SOCKS AND GLOVES: Pack them flat to fit in with the rest of the contents of the case. I roll socks only to put them in shoes, otherwise I leave them flat. The same goes for gloves, which I pack palm to palm. Pack nightclothes and underwear flat. According to Barbara, who is an expert at packing, stockings can be either rolled or laid flat.

SHOES: Pack low-heeled shoes with the uppers, not the soles, facing each other. If you are not taking shoe trees, stuff rolled-up socks or stockings in the toes. Pack high-heeled shoes one under the other to allow the heels to face inwards.

TIES: I never roll ties because they crease so badly if they are squashed. I prefer to pack them flat.

Lay ties flat in stacks of three or four, with the broad end face down on tissue paper. Fold the narrow ends over and wrap the tissue over the ties.

A soft silk tie needs special packing. Use tissue in the fold to prevent creasing. Wrap each tie in a separate parcel of tissue.

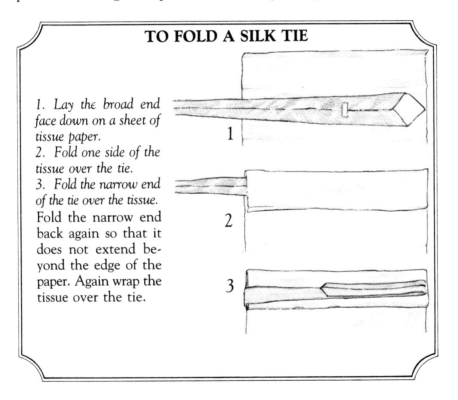

TO FOLD A SILK TIE

1. Lay the broad end face down on a sheet of tissue paper.
2. Fold one side of the tissue over the tie.
3. Fold the narrow end of the tie over the tissue. Fold the narrow end back again so that it does not extend beyond the edge of the paper. Again wrap the tissue over the tie.

SUNDRIES: The most practical sponge bag for a man is one with a drawstring. Squeeze all the air out of it to make it as thin as possible, wrap the string round the top, tie it, turn over the top and tie it again.

Pack men's brushes with the bristles together. In my day a gentleman had a leather brush case. The brush fitted snugly and there was a slot for the comb.

DIRTY LINEN: Most people return home with their dirty clothes rolled into a ball. This is a great waste of space. Everything should be folded as it was when it was clean, because then it doesn't take up any more room than when you first packed it.

When packing dirty clothes to go away again, lay them on the bottom of your case and put something, such as a sheet of tissue paper, over the top to protect your clean clothes.

Guests seldom stayed in a house long enough to use the private laundry, so they had to pack sufficient clean clothes for their visit. We had one guest who changed his clothes very often. He always arrived with two suitcases full of freshly laundered clothes that were packed as flat as if they had been sat on by an elephant. When he left, he had two suitcases full of dirty laundry to take away with him–fourteen or fifteen shirts, the same amount of underwear and heaven knows how many pairs of trousers. It all had to be folded and packed flat or it would never have fit into the cases. Nobody ever packed for him except me.

LOADING A CASE

Pack heavy clothes at the bottom of a case and lighter garments towards the top so that less weight bears on them.

TROUSERS: Put trousers at the bottom of the case, because they need to be flat. To protect the crease on the front trouser leg, let it face towards the handle of the case where less weight will bear on it.

SKIRTS: A lightweight skirt should lie near the top of the case, and a wool or tweed skirt is best placed flat at the bottom near the trousers.

JACKETS: Pack jackets after trousers or heavy skirts. Depending on the size of the case and the length of the jacket, it can perhaps lie between the back of the case and the handle with the collar facing towards the handle. If it is too large, lay it across the case, with the collar facing towards the center of the case and not pressed against the side.

SHIRTS: As shirts are light garments, put them near the top of your packing. If you do not have a shirt bag, lay them on clean underwear. Shirt collars crease more easily than reinforced jacket collars and must face towards the center of the case. Shirt fronts must be kept away from grease or anything else that might stain them, so do not pack them near shoes unless the shoes are covered.

DRESSES: Pack a soft dress near the top of your case and a heavy woolen dress near the bottom. For neat-looking packing, turn a dress over before you lay it in the case so that the front faces upwards.

SWEATERS: Most ordinary sweaters can fit in with the contours of everything else and can be used to fill gaps in your suitcase. Sweaters could also be wrapped round the soles of shoes to keep them from touching shirts or underwear. Pack fine sweaters more carefully near the top of your case.

LINEN, SOCKS AND GLOVES: These small items help keep packing in a firm block if they are laid flat and used to fill gaps.

TIES: Lay ties flat, either in a parcel of tissue paper (see page 103) or in a plastic shirt bag. Or lay them between your underwear or between your underwear and shirts. Always place them near the top of your case to prevent them from crushing.

SHOES: Depending on the gaps in the case, I often can fit a pair of low-heeled shoes in one of the back corners against a folded jacket shoulder. The soles of the shoes are facing, but not lying on, the trousers or skirt, and this helps keep them in position.

Pack a pair of high-heeled shoes in a corner, so that the heels rest against the side of the case and the uppers face towards the center of your packing. Wrap a pair of socks round the heels so that they can't damage the other garments. When I was a footman, we always wrapped shoes in tissue paper for traveling as shoe soles were kept highly polished. I prefer to use a shoe bag or to cover shoes with a sweater; plastic bags tear easily, brown wrapping paper is too stiff, and the ink from a newspaper will mark your clothes.

DRESSING GOWN: Pack a dressing gown as a protective covering over the rest of the items in the case. To do this, lay it flat in the case after everything but your raincoat has been packed. Fold it down around the contents of the case.

RAINCOAT: Although a raincoat is the last item to pack, the material is too stiff to be used to keep the packing tight. After you have folded the raincoat, tuck any extra material into the folds to keep the case tidy.

PACKING A HANGING BAG

I have never really approved of hanging bags, although I do own one. Packing clothes in hanging bags is a lazy man's way, and it is not a good way. They are, however, lightweight, and compact when empty. As with other types of luggage, there is a right way and a wrong way to pack a hanging bag.

If you are going to use one, lay it out flat on the floor. Shake the creases out of your garments as you take them from the wardrobe. Then lay the clothes on your bed so you can decide exactly what you need and determine the order of packing. I use wooden hangers from my wardrobe because the hangers supplied with hanging bags are so flimsy. I get down on my hands and knees to put the things in; I usually rearrange them after they are in the bag. Lay garments flat, making sure not to disturb the layers underneath.

SHOES: I pack my shoes before anything else. If shoes are packed in the center of the bag, they will create a large bump. I put them in the corners, so they will be at the top of the bag after it is folded up. The toes should be directly below the handle, or face towards it. After your jacket is packed they will lie above its shoulders; the uppers of low-heeled shoes will rest above them with the soles pressed against the case. The heels of high-heeled shoes should face inwards so that the uppers press against the case.

TROUSERS: When hanging a suit, hang the trousers first, then the waistcoat and jacket. To save wear, avoid folding trousers at the knee. The knee must not lie over the bar of the hanger, nor should it lie along the fold in the bag.

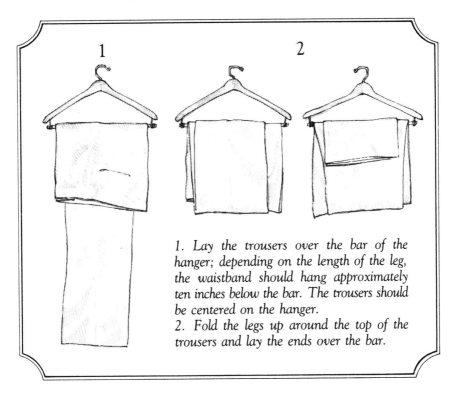

1. Lay the trousers over the bar of the hanger; depending on the length of the leg, the waistband should hang approximately ten inches below the bar. The trousers should be centered on the hanger.
2. Fold the legs up around the top of the trousers and lay the ends over the bar.

WAISTCOAT: A waistcoat should hang as flat as possible. Bring the buttonholes a third of the way over the pocket on the opposite side, so that the two bottom points overlap.

SHIRTS: I fold shirts, because they crumple more easily on hangers, and put them in an outside pocket of the bag where they lie flat. Pack shirts in a shirt bag or wrap them in tissue paper or sandwich them between clean underwear.

JACKET IN A HANGING BAG

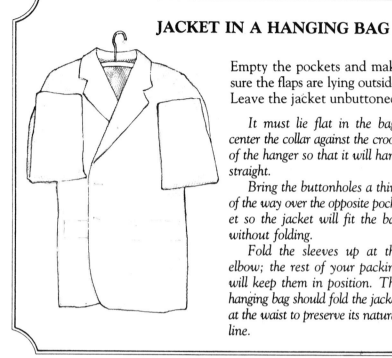

Empty the pockets and make sure the flaps are lying outside. Leave the jacket unbuttoned.

It must lie flat in the bag; center the collar against the crook of the hanger so that it will hang straight.

Bring the buttonholes a third of the way over the opposite pocket so the jacket will fit the bag without folding.

Fold the sleeves up at the elbow; the rest of your packing will keep them in position. The hanging bag should fold the jacket at the waist to preserve its natural line.

RAINCOAT: Because a raincoat is so bulky, take extra care to pack it flat. Take everything out of the pockets, making certain that the flaps are lying on the outside. Remove the belt, roll it and pack it separately. See that the center of the collar lies against the crook of the hanger so the raincoat will hang straight. Pull the vents down at the back.

Bring the buttonholes as far over as is necessary to allow the raincoat to fit the case without folding. Once it is in the case, smooth the lapels and fold the sleeves up at the elbows. Turn up any extra length at the bottom.

TIES: Fold (see page 103) and pack with shirts.

SWEATERS: Fold sweaters (see page 79) and lay them on top of suits or over wool skirts and dresses. I use my longest sweater to cover all my heavy clothing; it also keeps the rest of my sweaters in position. I lay it flat and tuck any extra material down around the contents of the bag.

SKIRT IN A HANGING BAG

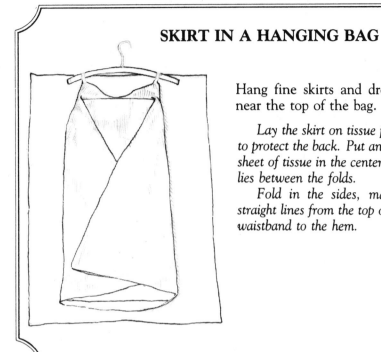

Hang fine skirts and dresses near the top of the bag.

Lay the skirt on tissue paper to protect the back. Put another sheet of tissue in the center so it lies between the folds.

Fold in the sides, making straight lines from the top of the waistband to the hem.

DRESSES: Lay a dress face up on tissue paper to protect the back. Cover the front with tissue paper to prevent creases. Fold the sleeves up at the elbow as for a jacket. Turn in the flares on the skirt. Fold up the bottom of the dress as necessary to fit the bag.

DRESSING GOWN: Unless you are packing a raincoat, put this in last to keep the packing together.

LINEN: Use underwear to fill gaps or pack it flat beneath the dressing gown.

SUNDRIES: Because there is so little safe storage space inside a hanging bag, I suggest you pack as few breakables as possible. Protect them in a pair of rolled-up socks or in a shoe. Tuck a man's sponge bag or woman's makeup bag in one of the corners; when the bag folds up, they will be at the top of the case by the handle.

DIRTY LINEN: Wrap it in tissue paper and put it in the outside pocket. If you pack it in the body of the case, put it in and cover it with a layer of tissue paper.

MANAGING THE TABLE

I believe that conversation is the essence of a party, what you eat and drink is the spice of it and a well-laid table hints of what is to come, like the wrapping on a present.

If you are going to arrange a special dinner, you must pay attention to detail. As far as we staff were concerned it didn't matter if it was one for dinner or twenty for dinner or four hundred to a party. The same attention to detail was expected, and everything was done the same way.

WINE AND SPIRITS

When I began in service, the amount of beer consumed by the gentlemen (and the older members of staff) was fantastic. Beer was delivered by horse and cart in ten-gallon barrels, and it seemed to me it arrived every day. The gentlemen drank light ale or draught beer before and during lunch; some drank pilsner or Barclays of London lager. Others had a martini before lunch (two parts gin and two parts vermouth). If the men were with the ladies, they'd have sherry to keep them company, and occasionally a gin and It (gin and Italian vermouth). The ladies certainly never drank beer.

Before dinner we served sherries or cocktails. We offered white wine with fish, red wine with meat and white wine and champagne with sweets. Then came the dessert wines–port, brown sherries and malmseys–and liqueurs after coffee. The grog tray was brought in about ten before everyone went to bed. It had everything on it–whiskey, gin and mixing brandy for more sophisticated travelers; soft drinks for the ladies, followed by a flask of hot water, which was a favorite nightcap of theirs.

Nowadays most people do not expect to be offered such a wide variety of drinks. I recommend an aperitif before a meal–not wine, because it is acidic. Wine should be drunk with a meal and a liqueur to digest it afterwards. But your selection of drinks of course depends on your taste and that of your guests.

SPIRITS

Tightly capped and stored upright, a bottle of spirits will last for a year after being opened. Spirits, whiskey especially, look best in a decanter. I never fill a decanter to the brim; one bottle is enough even if your decanter is particularly large. If it is too full, it will bubble and spurt when you pour.

I pour approximately one part whiskey or gin to two parts soda or water. I never measure quantities into a glass as though I were serving in a pub. I never fill a glass too full to be held comfortably;

about an inch of whiskey or gin is a generous measure in any glass. If I am serving an elderly man with a shaky hand, I give him less so he won't spill it. And if someone asks for a small, I give them exactly that because they can always have more.

In my day whiskey wasn't expensive and all the big houses had plenty. There was always whiskey on the table at breakfast, in little silver-topped decanters that held two gills (ten fluid ounces). The men put it on their porridge. Old George Summers, huntsman to the Buccleugh for about forty years, used to visit Barbara and me when he rode home from hunting. When he called at our cottage, we'd take three tots of whiskey out to him. He'd pour one in each boot and one down his neck to warm himself up for the rest of his journey.

COCKTAILS

There was a great deal of entertaining between the wars. It seemed that if people weren't giving a cocktail party, they were going out to one, and then they'd come in and want another lift-up. We served cocktails before dinner to the more sophisticated London ladies. But the ladies didn't drink as much as ladies do today, and most of them drank water at dinner.

WHITE LADY: One of the most popular cocktails was the White Lady. This is made with two parts dry gin, one part fresh passion fruit juice, a strong dash of Cointreau and plenty of cracked ice. Put it in a cocktail shaker and give it a vigorous shake. You can use fresh lemon or lime juice instead of passion fruit juice.

MARTINI: We served most gentlemen dry martinis. The trick of making a good martini is to cut a lemon in half or quarters and rub the cut surface round the rim of each glass. This gives the cocktail more of a bite. A dry martini is made with two-thirds gin and one-third dry white vermouth, with plenty of crushed ice. I crush the ice by wrapping it in a napkin and knocking it against a hard surface. I put the ice in first—six cubes to a quart-sized shaker. Then I add the gin and vermouth, screw on the top and give it a jolly good shake before pouring.

FRUIT CUPS AND PUNCHES

At tennis parties in the summer we sometimes served an iced fruit cup for tea, under one of the old copper beech trees on the lawn. At other times we served wine, or fruit cup with a little gin added.

ROYAL PUNCH: This punch is very potent; when making it, beware of the fumes arising with the steam. It is traditionally served on New Year's Eve. It is as well to buy inexpensive glasses for the occasion, as the custom is to hurl the glasses to the floor after the first toast to the New Year. It is wise to have a dust sheet on the floor for the quick removal of broken glass.

Brew two ounces of Indian tea in a quart of water. Pour a bottle of Burgundy into a large saucepan and heat it slowly over low heat. As soon as steam rises, add a bottle of hock; stirring, add a bottle of medium sherry and a bottle of rum. Mix the juice of six lemons with a pound of lump sugar and add to the wine mixture when it is near the boiling point. Pour the tea through a strainer into the simmering liquid. Finally add a pinch of ground ginger, a pinch of nutmeg and two sticks of cinnamon. Pour into a silver punch bowl and serve with a ladle in glasses of about claret size. The glasses should be warmed to lessen the risk of breakage.

SHERRY

Most sherries are served with the chill off them, but I pop the bottle in the fridge about half an hour before serving. You would be surprised at the difference; when it's cold, it's very much more palatable and refreshing.

WINE

A butler is the chief manservant in charge of the plate and the wine. Before a dinner party I would discuss the menu with my employer and advise him, if necessary. Then he would choose his wine, and I would get it out.

STORING WINE: The houses where I was in service had cellars where quantities of wine could be stored. These were built of stone, with stone bins to hold the wine. The bins might run a yard square and hold a solid square of bottles, perhaps ten across and ten high. But where you store wine and how you choose to lay it down depends on the number of bottles you own, the space you have available and how much you wish to spend.

Wine must be carefully preserved if it is to remain fit to drink. The bottles must lie flat so that the corks are kept moist and in good condition. The storage space should be dark to help the wine keep its color. Even a strong electric light can be harmful, so you would be wise to use a low wattage bulb. There must be some ventilation; if you are storing wine in a cupboard, you should probably bore a few one-inch holes in the door.

It must be stored at a cool even temperature, ideally between fifty and sixty degrees Fahrenheit, away from any source of heat. If the temperature fluctuates above seventy-five, it will shorten the lifespan of your wine, although the wine will not be destroyed.

The least cumbersome and most practical method of storing bottles of the same wine is to stack them in a cupboard. Lay a row of six bottles on the bottom of the cupboard, where it's coolest, with the corks facing outwards towards you. Roll a tea towel into the shape of a sausage and lay it across the necks for extra protection. Place five bottles on top so that each lies between two bottles in the bottom row. These should face the opposite way.

LAYING DOWN WINE: In order to give the sediment time to settle at the bottom, do not lay bottles down until a few days after purchase. When you lay them down, make sure all the labels face upwards for easy identification. This also keeps all the bottles at the same angle; if you take out a bottle and then return it un-opened, you can replace it in the same position. If you put it back at a different angle, the sediment will mix with the wine. I used to put a dab of paint on old bottles of wine that had no labels, so I knew which way they lay.

Make sure that the whites are placed on the bottom of your storage space, where it's coolest, and only the most substantial reds are placed on top. To avoid confusing one wine with another, be careful of the order in which you place your bottles. I always separate my hocks from my moselles, because the bottles are a similar shape. I might put my clarets and Burgundies between them; no one could confuse those, because a claret bottle is straight-sided and Burgundy has wide shoulders.

OPENING WINE: It is of the utmost importance to open a bottle of wine correctly. However superb the wine, the slightest trace of grit in your glass can completely ruin the taste.

I prefer a simple old-fashioned corkscrew with a single bar and wide handles. It is easy to use. All you have to do is screw it in and pull it out.

To open a sealed bottle of wine, begin by removing the seal from the cork. Then wipe the top and round the rim of the bottle with a cloth to remove any bits and pieces of wax or residue. Have a look to see how deeply the cork fits into the bottle before you start and compare this depth with the length of your corkscrew; this will enable you to judge when you have screwed it in far enough.

TO UNCORK WINE

If you are right-handed, hold the bottle in your left hand with your thumb against the shoulder and fingers round the neck. Stand up and put the bottle between your knees, with a cloth round it to protect your clothes in case it breaks. Hold the corkscrew in your right hand.

The corkscrew must go through the center of the cork, and it must be kept upright and straight. Most people break corks by putting the corkscrew in off-center and then trying again, which makes for an even larger hole. Turn the corkscrew gently all the way round, your wrist moving clockwise. When the corkscrew has nearly reached the bottom of the cork, bring it up carefully with a slight movement as if you were still turning it into the cork.

The sides of the cork are squeezed as it comes up; if there is any deposit on the cork, it could be left on the side of the bottle. After drawing the cork, wipe at least an inch under the lip to remove any sediment that has been left there. Use a clean cloth; the one that was wrapped round the bottle may have become dusty. I always examine the deposit on the cloth afterwards. It gives me some idea of the condition of the wine and of any other bottles of the same wine I have stored.

After opening a bottle of wine I smell the cork. This gives an indication of whether the wine is good or bad. If the cork has a musty smell, invariably the wine will have taken on a musty taste.

TASTING WINE: There are a number of reasons why wine might taste below par. White wine becomes acidic if it is kept in a warm atmosphere for too long. Wine can acquire a sugary taste through old age, and it may taste vinegary if air somehow seeped past the cork into the bottle while it was stored.

Lessen the risk of serving a flawed wine by tasting it first. Most people find it more helpful to taste than to smell wine, but I am experienced enough to judge it on the strength of my nose. In fact, my nose is infallible. If the cork smells musty or I am not happy with the bouquet, then I taste. Always smell before tasting, and taste two or three minutes after drawing the cork. The one should complement the other.

Before smelling or tasting wine, I put a couple of teaspoonfuls into a very thin clear glass and look at it. This is to check that it has no bits floating in it, which some less expensive wines tend to have, and that it is not cloudy. Wine may become cloudy because of a bad cask, because the bottling was wrong or if the bottle was dirty when the wine was first put in.

The glass should be held up to sunlight or electric light for a clear view. In a restaurant, you can hold the glass in front of a white tablecloth. If the wine looks wrong, you should ask for the wine waiter with a view to returning it. The same applies if it tastes wrong.

You must smell wine in a glass or you will smell the bottle, and a thin glass allows you to taste more accurately. When I smell wine I don't do anything fancy. I gently move the glass backwards and forwards beneath my nose and take perhaps two or three sniffs. The wine must move in the glass so you can inhale the whole bouquet. If you hold it still, you will only smell one side and not the entirety.

Now take a sip of the wine in your mouth and allow it to sit on your tongue. Savor it long enough to have a sensation of it. You are supposed to spit it out, but I always swallow a decent wine. **LETTING WINE BREATHE:** When wine is first drawn, there is a stiffness about it that softens with fresh air. Also, if you taste the wine a couple of hours before serving, you have time to change it if it isn't up to your standard.

I like to open rich red wines (Burgundies and Bordeaux) a couple of hours in advance. Light reds such as Beaujolais and all white wines should be allowed to breathe for at least fifteen minutes before serving. Young whites and rosés require only five or ten minutes. As they are to be served chilled, let them stand in a cool place. Be careful of very aged wines, twenty-five years or more, because they may spoil if allowed too much breathing space. It is wise to taste them upon opening. If the wine tastes mellow, it is ready to be consumed within half an hour. Otherwise it can be served after an hour or so.

DECANTING WINE: Wine should be decanted as soon as the bottle is opened. Practically speaking, there are three good reasons for decanting wine. First, it prevents sediment from mixing with the wine, which can make it bitter and in some cases undrinkable. Second, red wine can be more clearly seen in a decanter than in a bottle. And third, the process of transferring the wine aerates it thoroughly. In the better houses wine was always decanted.

A decanter should be filled to three-quarters full. To decant, hold the open bottle steady in your right hand, taking care not to disturb the sediment. Hold the decanter in your left. If the bottle is not transparent, place a strong light from a candle or electric bulb behind it, so you can observe the movement of the sediment.

Slowly pour the wine into the decanter, letting it flow down along the side. If you simply let the wine hit the bottom of the decanter, you would deprive it of oxygen.

STRAINING WINE: If you break a cork, you may have to push it into the bottle and strain the wine into a decanter. Personally, I would suggest erring on the side of caution and straining all wine, whether or not the cork has broken. Sediment-heavy wine should always be strained. I strain wine with a small pad of gauze, or a linen handkerchief doubled for extra thickness. A fine-meshed wine sieve can also be used. Whichever you choose, place it over the funnel of the decanter. Put a light behind the bottle so you can watch the sediment, then carefully decant as described.

WINE TEMPERATURE: To be fully enjoyed, wine must be served at the correct temperature. Serve red wine at room temperature, sixty-five to seventy-two degrees Fahrenheit. Let it breathe in the room where it is to be consumed. This is a gradual process; never warm wine quickly near a source of heat. Chill sweet white wine for two to three hours and serve at forty degrees Fahrenheit. Chill dry white wine for a couple of hours and serve at forty-five degrees. Older white wines should not be left in the refrigerator for longer than an hour and should never be served cooler than fifty-five degrees. Rosé should be chilled in the refrigerator and served at forty-five degrees.

STORING OPENED WINE: Once opened, wine–particularly sediment-heavy wine–absorbs tastes and odors from the atmosphere. For this reason, a bottle should be consumed within twenty-four hours or on two consecutive nights. Anything left over can be used for cooking; even then, I wouldn't keep it for longer than a week. Store it in a cool place–not in the fridge, which will make the wine too cold and destroy its bouquet.

CHAMPAGNE

Champagne should be uncorked with the greatest of care and treated very gently, because it is very much alive. After carefully undoing the wires, put your thumb underneath the cork lip and ease up gently. As soon as you feel the cork beginning to yield, firmly take hold of the top, give it a half turn and pull upwards slowly and smoothly. Be certain to turn the cork anticlockwise, because your grip is stronger inwards than outwards. As soon as the cork is released–not popped–wipe the inside lip with a damp cloth. This will keep the bubbles back.

We always poured champagne into a special jug. It was easier to serve from, and the pouring took the fizz away, which pleased the ladies. The jug was an elongated tulip shape, bulbous at the bottom, with a narrow funnel to let the gas escape. A full champagne jug was a marvelous sight.

The ideal temperature to drink champagne or any sparkling wine is forty degrees Fahrenheit. Simply chill it in the refrigerator for two to two and a half hours before serving. Then pour it out very gently indeed, letting it trickle into the glass. The glass should be two-thirds full. I prefer a shallow champagne glass that lets the fizz escape. If you wish to flatten the champagne further, swish it with a swizzle stick or the prongs of a silver fork.

All sparkling wines and champagnes are ready to drink the day they are bought. For storage, lay bottles down to keep the corks moist. Champagne should be kept cool, so put it at the bottom of your wine rack or cupboard.

PORT

Port is a fortified wine, an ordinary wine that began life similar to a Burgundy but was then laced with brandy. It is a dessert wine, and dessert wines are traditionally enjoyed with fruit before coffee and liqueurs are served. The other two main dessert wines are brown sherry and Madeira, although brown sherry is rarely served now. Several varieties of Madeira are produced; each is named after the type of grape used to make the wine. Malmsey, made from the Malvoisie grape, is the most popular. If you suffer from gout and can no longer drink port, malmsey will not upset you.

In Britain it is still customary for ladies to leave gentlemen over their port and to be joined by them later for coffee and liqueurs. In my day it wasn't considered right for ladies to drink port, except for half a glass with a dry biscuit in mid morning. This is very sustaining, and we were always ready to serve it. Lighter-bodied luncheon or tawny port was served at lunch in winter. Fine port was never taken on shooting lunches because it doesn't travel well. It needs to be treated with a great deal of care and never shaken, as it's very heavy-bodied.

All port should be laid down in the same way as wine. It too likes a dark storage place and an even temperature; it should be kept at fifty degrees Fahrenheit. The cork is drawn from port in the same manner as it is from wine, but it is firmer and more difficult to pull.

STRAINING PORT: Because port is sediment-heavy, it is not trustworthy enough to be consumed straight out of the bottle. I always strain it into a decanter. Strain port as you would strain a crusty wine (see page 119). At the finish hold the decanter up to the light; the port should be ruby red, bright and clear.

LETTING PORT BREATHE: All dessert wines very easily absorb cigarette or cigar smoke and lose their bouquet. Because port is a heavy-bodied wine and will absorb whatever is in the air, it must be allowed to breathe in the decanter in a clean atmosphere. I never left an open decanter in the dining room because the gentlemen sometimes had a drink there before dinner; if they smoked, nonsmokers could taste it in their port. In my day no one smoked until the port had been drunk and the stopper returned to the decanter. One still does not smoke at a public dinner until after the Royal Toast, when the Master of Ceremonies announces, "Gentlemen, you may smoke."

SERVING PORT: Port is served from the right, and after the decanter is restoppered it is placed on the right-hand side of the host. There is an old superstition that bad luck will fall on the table unless port is passed clockwise, so if a man refuses port and then changes his mind, the decanter must go all the way round the table again to reach him. At one time it was considered a slight to the host to refuse his port.

STORING OPENED PORT: Port should be drunk within a week of being decanted, because by then it will have absorbed different tastes from the atmosphere. But as a decanter holds only a bottle, which is six to six and a half glasses, it should be possible to consume it within my time limit.

BRANDY

Brandy is made from distilled wine, and the name comes from the Dutch words meaning "burnt wine." Fine brandies should be drunk neat. Mixing brandy, which is of lesser quality and cost, should be mixed with two parts soda or water to one part brandy.

Mr. Dunkels, one of my employers, had a three-foot-high cognac bottle. It held three magnums of one of the finest brandies—a hundred-year-old Napoleon. This was a rich amber color, smooth and mellow to taste. You had to be a strong man to take it round the table; I carried it in two arms. Everybody laughed when this huge bottle was brought into the dining room and they were offered a drop of brandy. It was poured straight into brandy rummers.

LIQUEURS

A liqueur is a digestive. If you have eaten a hearty dinner which has left you feeling full and flatulent, a liqueur should help at once. Different liqueurs suit different people. Personally, I find the best liqueur to remove overfullness is orange Curaçao.

Liqueurs are potent, and one glass is sufficient to digest any meal on this earth. Admittedly a liqueur glass is small, one-third the size of a sherry glass. But any more than this will produce a liverish, depressed feeling.

THE MORNING AFTER

If you're suffering from a bad hangover, drink a sherry glass full of port and brandy in equal measures. It's fairly potent but especially good if you've got a loose bowel movement. Half a glass of Tio Pepe, which is a very dry sherry, sometimes helps. Another cure is a few drops of Angostura bitters in a glass of tonic water.

LAYING THE TABLE

You should have nothing to worry about during dinner; everything should be ready well beforehand–flowers on hand, wine chosen, food prepared. Allow yourself plenty of time for preparation. I feel you should always have new candles, freshly laundered napkins and clean silver. Make sure you have enough clean cutlery to replace any that might accidentally fall on the floor or slip into a serving dish. See that none of your plates are cracked or chipped; polish plates after taking them out of the cupboard (see page 159). Do the same with your glasses when laying them on the table (see page 160); they should be left gleaming and not handled again until they are filled with wine.

If you customarily give dinners for six, you should have enough place settings for eight, because invariably things will be lost or broken. For your own peace of mind have more than one replacement; if somebody drops a fork on the floor, you shouldn't have to go out and wash it, then bring it back.

In my view, six serving spoons and six serving forks is the minimum you should have. Ideally you should lay out more serving spoons and forks than you think you will need. There are some very clumsy people about–while they are talking, they let go of the vegetable spoon and it slides into the dish. You don't want to fish it out; it's much better to leave it in and use another. Also, it is surprising how many people will take the spoon out of the peas and replace it in the beans, leaving one dish with two spoons in it and the other without any. You can't take a spoon out of the beans and put it back in the peas in front of a nice guest; you leave two spoons in the beans and provide a clean spoon for the peas.

SEATING

Always arrange the chairs before laying the table so you can organize your place settings in relation to them.

A frequent error of new footmen was to misplace the chairs round the table. Seating must be planned so that your guests are sitting directly opposite one another. Supposing you had seven to seat round an oval table; it would look a bit silly to seat three on one side, two on another and one at each end, as you would for rectangular table. The host should sit at the top, two guests on each side, and two at the bottom. The chairs should be approximately half a yard out from the table so it will be easy for your guests to seat themselves. There must be sufficient space between the chairs; sit on one of the chairs yourself to see how much elbow room you have allowed. If you are being waited upon, allow enough room between the chairs for the person who is serving to lean forward and reach down to the side of your plate. If you are doing the serving, remember to sit where you can easily leave the table. Avoid using any chair that squeaks. All these things count and make an evening flow smoothly.

A well-planned seating arrangement can contribute a great deal to the success of a dinner. The primary considerations are ease, protocol and conversation.

Something as obvious as your guests' physical comfort should not be overlooked. For example, if you put a tremendously large man in the middle of a small table, he would take up all the room and cramp the ladies next to him. Instead, put him near the end.

As a matter of protocol, the leading guest should sit on the hostess's right and his wife should sit on the host's right. When royalty were entertained, they sat at either end of the table in place of the host and hostess. The host and hostess were seated to their left, so that they still kept royalty on their right. I found that officially a bishop or archbishop took the hostess's place and she sat on his right. Unofficially they didn't seem to stand on their dignity.

Once your honored guests are placed, seat for conversation and interest. You wouldn't put a hunting man with a fashion designer. If you had a designer of ladies' clothes, you could put him with an interior decorator. What you must never do is seat a couple of teenagers next to a couple of fusty old grandfathers. They don't go together. The old men have nothing to say to the youngsters, because they have nothing in common, and the youngsters certainly don't want to talk to the old men.

In the old days a gentleman was waited on when he dined alone, but he never ate in solitary splendor at the head of a long dining room table—that's another of those fictions. Either we made the table shorter or he sat at a small table somewhere else. When the gentleman and lady were alone together, we shortened the table and they sat together at one end, not halfway across the room from each other. They were quite sensible down-to-earth people.

TABLE LINEN

In my day a lace tablecloth was used on the outside buffet table at a garden party or for tea at a birthday party, when the nannies stood behind the children's chairs. Personally, I don't think a lace cloth is suitable for lunch or dinner and would still only use it for tea.

You cannot go wrong with a white tablecloth, preferably damask or Irish linen. Damask napkins and tablecloths last at least forty years, which makes their cost seem more reasonable. We always used matching white damask tablecloths and napkins. The housekeeper gave us the appropriate size when a party was being held. Sixteen guests meant a thirty-two-foot tablecloth was required.

Any cloth napkin is infinitely preferable to a paper one. Paper napkins cannot be folded elegantly (see page 135); in any case, I think they look both limp and cheap.

Your tablecloth should have enough overhang so that it doesn't look skimpy. It should fall approximately halfway to the floor. Make sure that the center crease is dead in the middle of the table. You must have baize underneath the tablecloth to protect the table. Baize will also give the cloth a much fuller appearance and keep it in place.

A warm plate or dish will melt the polish on a polished table and leave an ugly ring, so if you are not using a cloth you must protect the surface with table mats. Without a cloth, a well-polished table will reflect your silver beautifully, but a tablecloth has the advantage of hiding the join if you've put on extra leaves. Also, if there is no cloth, wine bottles and decanters must stand on coasters so as not to leave sticky rings, and a water jug should be set on a glass plate to prevent it from marking the table.

A tablecloth, especially a white one, will show wear. Its freshness will go, it will pick up telltale crumbs, creases in the wrong place or smudges of ash. When I was in service, we changed the tablecloth whenever it was marked, which might have been three times a day. And we never used a cloth more than twice before washing, which I still think is enough. In the old days we never used the same napkin twice; nowadays, I feel that a napkin can be used again at a family meal, provided it has stayed clean. I change a napkin that is soiled or crumpled even if it has only been used once. Tablecloths and napkins should always be laundered before storing, even if they have been used only once and appear clean.

CENTERPIECE

Whatever is going on dead center goes on the table first. The centerpiece is the most important thing on the table, as it is the first thing that catches one's attention. It should not be so high that it is awkward to talk over, and it must be in proportion to the candlesticks.

Fruit makes an attractive centerpiece, with the added advantage that it can be eaten through dinner. Always put soft fruit near the top to prevent it from being squashed. Particularly if you are having cherries, polish the fruit to give it added gloss. Polish fruit with a clean napkin or freshly laundered tea cloth, the softer the better. I polish mine with a napkin; I cradle the fruit inside the napkin in my left hand and, using the same napkin, briskly polish it with my right hand. After I have polished it, I never touch it again with my bare hand.

I also like a flower arrangement with a variety of colors, in small flower vases or a bowl. Flowers should not be too strongly scented, as this might interfere with the aroma of the food. We always had flowers in the castle, and I used to arrange them for the centerpiece.

When I was footman in London and there was a special party on, flowers were brought up from the country by our own van or by train. The butler found out from the lady's maid what color gown the lady was wearing that night, and I would go to Covent Garden early in the morning to buy flowers that matched her dress, even if they were out of season. When everything was ready and the table laid, the lady would come down–as she said–to admire it, although she really came to check on the flowers.

LIGHTING THE TABLE

Candlesticks are arranged on either side of the centerpiece or at each corner. Each place setting should be well lit by candlelight alone; generally, four candles should be enough for six place settings and six candles for eight. At a dinner for two, two candle-sticks is enough–any more would be overdoing it, like wearing two waistcoats. Make sure the candles are not too high, so guests don't feel they are in the way of conversation. If the centerpiece consists of three candelabras, the center one should be the highest.

With candlelight over the table, you will need dim light for service. Picture lights, wall lights or one side lamp could be left on to serve by. I never like seeing a huge chandelier full on over the table; if a room is fully lighted, the candles lose their glow and their purpose. Before electric light we had candelabras on the serving table so we could see what we were doing. On the wall were silver sconces that held three or four shaded candles, and the light bounced off the silver back into the room.

I always put the service lights out when they were no longer necessary and taught my junior staff to do the same. But when one of the Mount parlormaids did this after she left us to go to Colonel Bolitho, he shouted at her. His butler had always left the service lights on, and he wasn't used to having them put out. He said he couldn't see what he was eating–although in fact he had more or less finished. What he really needed was someone like me to deal with. He wouldn't accept a new procedure from her, as she was inexperienced, but he would have accepted it from me.

Candles were used only on the dinner table. We never had

candles at lunchtime, no matter how large the table was or how important the lunch party was. The candlesticks were removed; if we thought the table looked bare, we could use another two pieces of silver or small vases of flowers to balance the centerpiece.

I believe in plain white candles, for every occasion. The candles should be slightly longer than the candlestick is tall. For an elegant table your candles must look perfect. I always buy new candles when we are having a party.

NEW CANDLES: How fast a new candle will light depends on the composition of the wick and on whether the wick is dry. It is wise to keep candles in a dry place. Waiting for a wick to flame may be a matter of only twenty or thirty seconds, but if you have six candles to light with only one match and you don't want to burn your fingers, you've got to move quickly.

If you slightly char the wicks of new candles in advance, they will flame at once when you come to light them. We used to char the candles for the dinner table in the morning so that we could light them immediately before announcing dinner.

PUTTING CANDLES OUT: I've seen chaps who couldn't blow out a candle and others who blew wax all over the table. We never blew out candles; we squeezed the flames with damp fingers. Squeezing the flame puts the candle out and doesn't get wax all over. It is a good idea to dip your forefinger and thumb into a finger-bowl before squeezing the flame, because your fingers must be fairly wet to protect them from being burnt. A lot of people put a hand behind the flame and then blow out the candle, but this can still let wax escape at the sides. We didn't make extra work for ourselves —there were consequences if I caught anyone blowing on a candle!

The last person to leave a room should always put out the candles. It is a guest's obligation to do this if the host has forgotten. We always used to listen for the gentlemen to leave the dining room so if the candles were still lit we could put them out at once. If we thought the men had been too long over their port, we might make a little bit of noise outside, just to remind them that we hadn't gone to bed yet, that we were still there and that we still had to clear up the dining room.

PREVENTING DRIPPING WAX: It is a good idea to buy small glass saucers that are designed to slip on top of candlesticks to catch the dripping wax and protect the candlestick and the table. And as glass is transparent, these saucers are not at all noticeable. Another good way of preventing drips (or "swalings," as we called them) is to sharpen the candle like a pencil. This eliminates the hollow where wax collects. Both the hollow and the swalings on the candle are unsightly, and a candle without swalings looks completely fresh when repointed. Pare candles when they're cold because the grease will flake off more easily; when it's warm and still malleable, the candle grease will stick on everything.

TO PARE A CANDLE

Hold the candle between the forefinger and thumb of your left hand. Take a sharp knife in your right hand and grip it between your forefinger and thumb, your thumb resting on the candle. Keep the knife still and turn the candle round against the knife blade. First cut away the edges of the hollow to create a flat surface all the way round the top of the candle. When you've removed the hollow and the top is absolutely flat, sharpen the candle like a pencil from a quarter of an inch below the flat surface. Point the candle as it was pointed when it was new. If there is an extra long piece of wick, cut it off. Two candles should take about five minutes to do.

REMOVING WAX: If wax does get on the table or tablecloth, there is a way to remove it. Warm a knife over the candle flame, gently slip it under the wax and lift the wax off the surface.

CONDIMENTS

In the old days a new footman's most common mistake in laying the table was to place the salts and peppers out of reach and out of line. Salt and pepper, and mustard if needed, should be near at hand. No one should have to get up or stretch across the table. Ideally there should be salt, pepper and mustard between two place settings. The salt and pepper should be parallel, with the mustard in front. The salt spoon should lie across the salt cellar with the handle facing towards the people who will use it. If none of the dishes will require mustard, I would put only one mustard pot between the hostess and her guest at either end of the table.

A wooden pepper mill is out of place on a formally set table. If everything else is silver, the pepper mill should be silver too.

I dislike seeing sauce bottles on a table. If the sauces must be there, I would put them in sauceboats. However, I feel that if someone has cooked a meal properly, you shouldn't need extra flavoring from a bottle.

Offer cream and sugar at the appropriate time, regardless of whether you think they are necessary, as your guests may want them and be embarrassed to ask. When sugar is offered in a castor or shaker, many people put sugar all over the table; they sprinkle it wildly and it flies everywhere. Avoid this by using a sugar basket or bowl with a spoon, so your guests can help themselves without making a mess.

ASHTRAYS

I also dislike seeing ashtrays on a table during the meal. I feel they unbalance the place setting. In my day we never laid ashtrays; it would have been considered the height of bad manners for anyone to have had a cigarette before the stopper was put back on the port decanter at the end of a meal. But things have changed to such an extent that people now smoke between courses. For guests who smoke, I would put one ashtray between two people, in line with the mustard in front of the salt and pepper. Ashtrays should be changed between courses. They should be replaced with clean ones or washed, not merely emptied and put back.

PLACE SETTINGS

It doesn't matter how much a table is altered during a meal; what counts is the effect it creates the first time you see it. There is a way of laying a table well. It must be balanced, and the place settings must be in line with the centerpiece and candlesticks. Footmen had to learn this. A new footman could never arrange a place setting accurately the first time, but would have to stand back and look at it from a better perspective, then alter it. I have seen a footman measure with a tape measure to lay the settings correctly. But a person like me, who has laid tables so often and for so long, can rely on the eye to match everything up with the centerpiece.

In my day the lady of the house would not interfere with how we laid the table; she wouldn't dream of it. Once I did have to take a young lady to task because she tried it. I had laid the table and gone home for tea. When I came back, I saw that things on the table had been moved, and I asked her if she had done it. "I thought I'd rearrange things, and then I tried to put them back," she replied.

I was an experienced servant and she was a young lady of twenty-four or twenty-five, and I wasn't going to have it. So I said, "If you want to lay the table, you lay the table. But don't you ever alter my table. If you want something moved, ask me to move it."

CUTLERY

In my day a large knife was known as a dinner knife and a small knife as a cheese knife. I still use those names; even though a cheese knife is used for a variety of things, I would never call it a bread knife or a butter knife. To me, a bread knife is a sword knife with a long blade that is used for slicing bread. A butter knife is a small knife kept by the butter dish and used for spreading butter.

The most proper way to eat fish in Britain is with two large forks. This is done on formal occasions, and I believe it still applies at Buckingham Palace. Until the 1914-18 war special knives and forks were used for fish in all the big houses. In those days, fish smelled so strong when it came out of the icehouse–there were no refrigerators then–that it would leave a fishy taste on the cutlery. Queen Mary supposedly was responsible for the new standard that it was correct to eat fish with two forks. As the story goes, she saw fish knives and forks on the dinner table in a working-class home. Because ordinary people seemed to be using fish knives and forks, they weren't used at the palace again. The aristocracy caught on to the idea; gentlemen used only a fork on fish, and if the fish was ticklish to debone, they used two. Only one fish fork was ever laid, but there was always a second fork handy for the meat course, which followed, and if it had been used for fish it was replaced.

We served six or seven courses at dinner, so we only laid the table as far as the main course; otherwise, there was too much on the table. Cutlery for the remaining courses was brought in as needed. Today, most people serve only two or three courses, and the table can be completely laid in advance.

Cutlery is arranged on the table in the order in which the pieces will be used. Knives and spoons are always on the right; forks are always on the left next to the side plate. If a fork is to be used for a starter, it would go outside the dinner fork on the left side. If you were starting with soup, the soupspoon would be outside the dinner knife on the right-hand side. The dessertspoon is inside the large knife, and the cheese knife is inside the dessertspoon. Leave enough space for the dinner plate between the knives and the forks, although the plate should be kept hot and not laid down until you are ready to eat off it. All knives and forks should be lying straight and level with one another; nothing looks more untidy than a spoon that is slightly higher than the rest of the place setting, or a knife handle that is lower than everything else.

To avoid leaving fingermarks on cutlery when laying the table, hold the pieces on the balance. This is the narrowest point of the handle—just above the blade of a knife, the prongs of a fork and the bowl of a spoon.

You can save time when laying the table by placing two knives, two spoons, or two forks at one go. Say you are having six people to dinner and you are laying forks. Hold six large forks stacked in your left hand and six dessert forks stacked in your right, because dessert forks will go inside the large forks. Palms downwards, hold the forks on the balance between your forefingers and thumbs. Hold your hands close together—there should be only a sixteenth of an inch between the two forks—and gently drop the bottom one off each stack. Then position your hands at the next place setting. When laying knives, you must leave an inch and a half between the cheese knife and the dinner knife for the bowl of the dessertspoon.

It doesn't matter whether you lay knives or forks first, but it is easier to lay the knives before laying the spoons. If you are laying only dessertspoons, hold them as described and drop each between two knives. If you are laying soupspoons also, hold them in your right hand and the dessertspoons in your left, and have your hands far enough apart to place the spoons on either side of the dinner knife. I don't like to see a dessertspoon and fork crossed above a place setting. Nine times out of ten this looks untidy. Furthermore, your salad plate may go there.

SALAD PLATE

If you eat salad with the main course, as we do in England, the salad plate should always be above the dinner plate. You cannot balance the table setting by putting the salad plate next to the side plate on the left, and if you put it on the right it is awkward and will crowd your peppers and salts. A half-moon plate is ideal, because it fits snugly round the dinner plate.

NAPKIN

The napkin should be laid in the space where the dinner plate will be, between the knives and the forks, or on the side plate. You should never put a napkin in a wineglass. If the napkin is not on the side plate you can put rolls of bread there instead, but I think bread tastes fresher if it is handed. I prefer not to put food on the table until my guests are seated, even if there is a first course that is to be served cold.

To fold napkins, see pages 135-143.

GLASSES

Lay glasses last, so you won't knock them over. They should be to the right, slightly above the point of the dinner knife. Allow at least an inch between the knife and the nearest glass, so that when the knife is picked up it won't clink against the glass. The glasses should also be far enough from the edge of the table and from the next place setting so that they are not hit when the person to the right is served.

In the old days we laid a sherry glass first, with a wineglass behind it and slightly to the right. Behind it and slightly to the left was a goblet, in case anyone wanted water or whiskey and soda with the meal. The wineglass was placed at an angle to the sherry glass so it was not in the way when sherry was poured. The goblet stood high enough to be reached over the other glasses. Nowadays, glasses should be arranged from front to back in order of use. Lay a glass for each wine, with a water goblet behind and to the left of them. If you are serving two wines and champagne, you might put the champagne glass behind the others, or provide the champagne glasses after the wineglasses are removed.

When laying glasses, it is best to have them on a tray that you can rest between two place settings. I always had a footman walking behind me with a salver.

There is a trick to picking up small wineglasses without chinking or marking them. Palm upwards, slip your first finger and middle finger around the stem of the glass. Support the bowl on the back of your thumbnail and the crook of your first finger. Extend your middle finger so the back of your fingernail can steady the foot of the glass. With practice, you can pick up two at a time, as we did: holding the first glass, pick up a second between your third finger and little finger. The first glass will be higher than the second. They don't chink because your thumb is between them, and they don't mark because only your thumbnail touches the first glass.

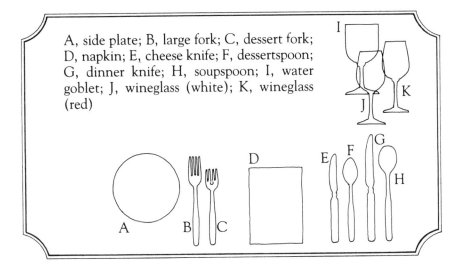

A, side plate; B, large fork; C, dessert fork; D, napkin; E, cheese knife; F, dessertspoon; G, dinner knife; H, soupspoon; I, water goblet; J, wineglass (white); K, wineglass (red)

FOLDING NAPKINS

To my mind a simple square looks attractive on any table. I don't go in for very elaborate folds; excessive folding can leave a napkin looking used, and I prefer to keep napkins clean. Because a napkin must look fresh, practice the folds before you finally use them. There's nothing worse than a napkin falling out of its fold.

When folding, be firm and deft so as not to crumple the napkin more than you have to. Use your thumb or palm to press the crease in at each stage. When there are many thicknesses, clench your hand and forcibly apply the side of your fist to the fold.

Napkins for folding should be approximately twenty-four to twenty-six inches on a side. They must first be slightly starched and smoothly pressed into a plain fold.

THE PLAIN FOLD

1

2

3

1. Lay the napkin flat.
2. Fold down one-third of the napkin.

3. Turn the napkin over. The fold should face towards you.

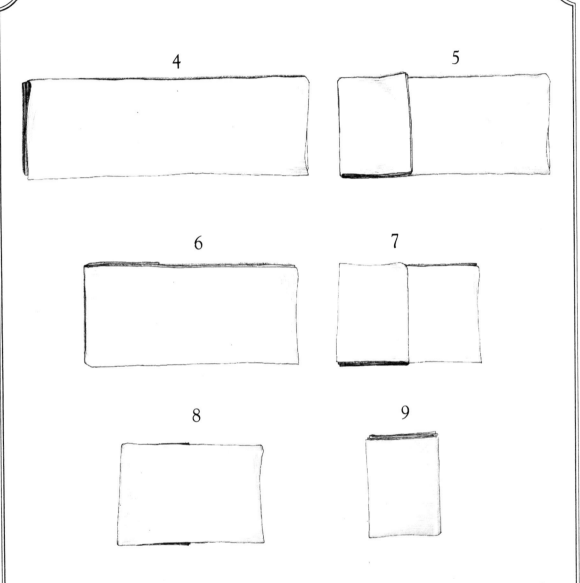

4. Bring the bottom edge even with the top.
5. Fold the left edge in to the center.
6. Turn the napkin over, keeping the fold on the left side.
7. Again fold the left edge to the center.

8. Again turn the napkin over, keeping the fold on the left side.
9. Fold the napkin in half. Give it a final press.
The plainly folded napkin can now be folded into a variety of shapes.

THE LAZY FOOTMAN

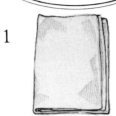
1

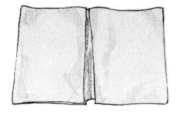
2

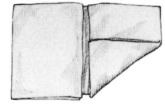
3

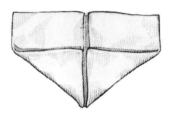
4

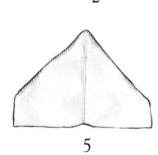
5

6

7

8

My favorite fold is known as the Lazy Footman. It is extremely easy to do, and I used it every day. I could walk round the table with six napkins under my arm, folding as I went.

1. Lay the plainly folded napkin on the table.
2. Open the last fold. If the center crease shows, turn the napkin over.
3. Bring the lower right-hand corner to the center in an angled fold.
4. Repeat on the left side.

5. Turn the napkin over so the center crease is face up. The point of the triangle should be at the top and the base facing towards you.
6. Pick up the napkin and slip the right end into the corner of the left end.
7. Turn the napkin top to bottom. There should be a neat fold at the back where the two ends of the base are firmly tucked into each other.
8. Stand the napkin on its base and you have a Lazy Footman. If necessary, you can make it look less stiff by gently tapping the front.

THE FOX'S MASK

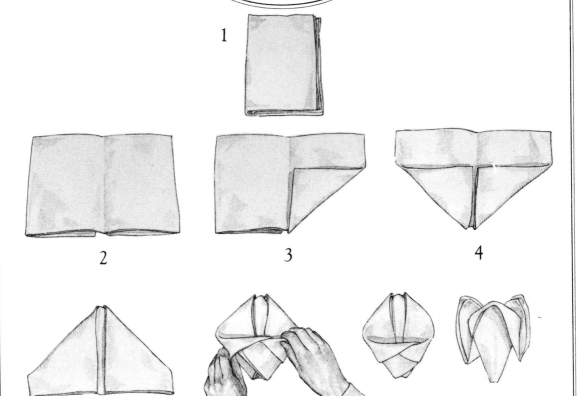

1. Lay the plainly folded napkin on the table.
2. Open the last fold, but this time make sure the center crease is face up.
3. Bring the lower right-hand corner to the center in an angled fold.
4. Repeat on the left side.
5. Turn the napkin over. The point of the triangle should be at the top and the base facing towards you.

6. Pick up the napkin and slip the right end of the base into the corner of the left end.
7. The two ends of the base should be firmly tucked into each other.
8. Instead of standing the napkin on its base, stand it on its back to form the fox's nose. Pull back the two flaps above it to give the fox some ears.

THE BISHOP'S MITER

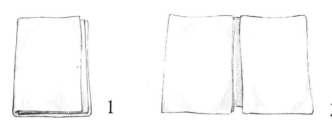

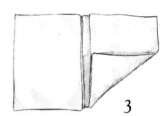

1

2

3

A   B

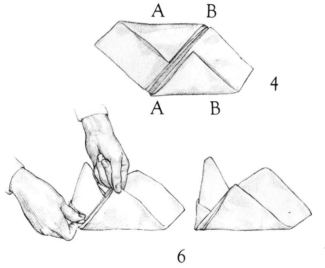

4

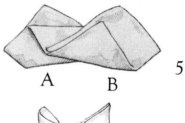

A   B

5

A   B

6

7

8

Some people stick a roll into a napkin folded this way, but we certainly never did.

1. Lay the plainly folded napkin on the table.
2. Open the last fold so the center crease is not face up.
3. Bring the lower right-hand corner to the center in an angled fold.
4. Bring the upper left-hand corner to the center in an angled fold.

5. Pick up the napkin and fold it away from you so that the two sides marked AB match and are parallel. The two points marked A should meet and the two points marked B should meet.
6. Fold the left-hand corner towards you and tuck it behind the front triangle.
7. Fold the right-hand corner away from you and tuck it behind the back triangle.
8. The Bishop's Miter is complete.

THE DUTCH HAT

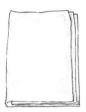

1

2

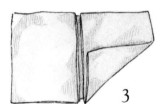

3

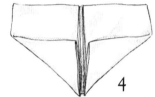

4

5

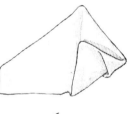

6

7

8

9

The beginning folds of the Dutch Hat are also similar to the Lazy Footman.

1. *Lay the plainly folded napkin on the table.*
2. *Open the last fold so the center crease is not face up.*
3. *Fold the lower right-hand corner to the center in an angled fold.*
4. *Repeat on the left side.*

5. *Turn the napkin over so the center crease is face up. The point of the triangle should be at the top, the base facing towards you.*
6. *Fold the lower right-hand corner to the center crease.*
7. *Repeat on the left side.*
8. *Fold on the center crease.*
9. *Stand the hat up on its base.*

THE FLEUR-DE-LIS

1

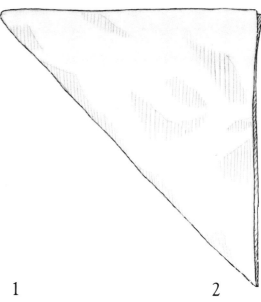

2

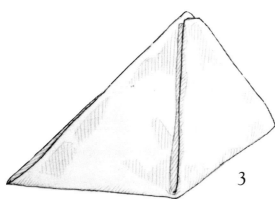

3

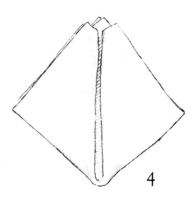

4

1. Unfold the napkin and lay it flat on the table.
2. Fold it into a triangle.

3. Fold the lower right-hand corner to the top of the triangle.
4. Repeat on the left side. The two sides should come close together so that the bottom point is sharp.

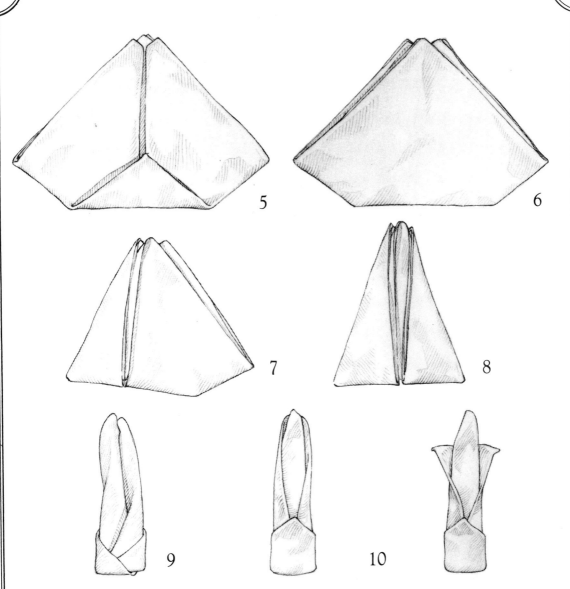

5. Fold the lowest point to the middle of the napkin. This will form a small triangle.

6. Turn the napkin over. The point should still be at the top.

7. Fold the left long side to the center crease.

8. Repeat on the right side to form a triangle.

9. Pick up the napkin and fold the two corners towards you. Tuck the right end into the left fold.

10. Pull out the tall folds on either side of the center. The Fleur-de-Lis is complete.

SERVING WELL

I first learnt to serve by waiting on the younger staff in the servants' hall when I was hallboy. I was always running around during meals; the hallboy was the last one to sit down and the first one to get up. As soon as the staff finished their meat, the hallboy had to serve them pudding, so I always ate quickly because I wanted to get as much as I could before being disturbed. The younger servants, from the housemaids and footmen downwards, were not allowed to speak during meals. We kept silent as though in a monastery.

At lunchtime the senior members of the staff left the servants' hall after the main course and ate their sweet in the steward's room or the housekeeper's room; they always ate dinner separately in one of these rooms. When the hallboy was promoted to steward's room boy, he waited on them there. And when the time came that the steward's room boy was allowed into the dining room, all he was permitted to take round the table was a toast rack. This went on for a month or so, until he could be trusted to carry round the plates and perhaps serve the sauces. Only after a long while was he considered competent enough to help out when one of the footmen was off duty.

When I started in 1922, protocol was very strict, but gradually it relaxed. Following the second war, household staffs became smaller, and everything was far less formal. When I became butler, I made the junior and senior staff eat together. The presence of the senior staff prevented the housemaids from complaining about the food, which upset the kitchen people needlessly. The housemaids gave far more trouble over what they ate than did the people they served!

My footmen were trained quite differently than I was. I would take a boy into the dining room his first night, provided I could find a suit for him. We would have two or three rehearsals round the dining room table beforehand, so during dinner he could just put out some plates and watch the rest of us.

SERVING

Serving is a straightforward business. The whole object is to be very unobtrusive, so people hardly realize you are there. We tried to be very quiet, which is the hallmark of professional service. We walked softly and never spoke to to one another; if we needed to communicate, we gestured. I always taught a new footman to walk clockwise round a table and never to turn back, because a collision could result if there was someone walking behind him.

We never served with a napkin over one arm; this may be done in restaurants, but it is not done in a dining room. And we stopped serving in white gloves at the end of the first war. Instead we wore special thumb napkins wrapped round our thumbs, so they wouldn't be seen while we were handling the plates or dishes. The butler inspected our fingers for cleanliness before each meal.

PLATES: The secret to serving well lies in a strong wrist and a firm grasp. I taught my footmen to carry a stack of plates before I allowed them to carry heavy serving dishes. When they became more experienced, they were able to carry twelve plates at a time, but it is wise to begin with four or five at most.

Food is always served from the left, and drink is always served from the right. A single plate should be held in the left hand so it is easy to place in front of the person being served. A stack of plates should be held in the right hand so the plates can be positioned with the left.

Hold a stack of plates in the palm of your right hand, your fingers spread out under the bottom plate. The palm of the hand should be near the edge of the bottom plate, and your thumb should stretch up the side of the plates to the rim of the top plate. Hold the pile steady with your left hand.

To take a plate off a pile of plates, push the top plate with your right thumb and slip the fingers of your left hand under the rim, pulling the plate gently onto the palm of that hand. Steady it with the side of your left thumb.

TO HOLD A PLATE

To hold a plate professionally, you should hold it on the palm of your hand, your fingers firmly gripping the bottom. Support it by resting the ball of your thumb against the rim, so only the outer edge of your thumb is visible. You must avoid leaving fingermarks, and your thumb must never go over the rim onto the side of the plate because this is where the mustard is put.

When you put the plate down, slide it from your left hand into position on the table. This is very easy to do. Lay the far side of the rim on the table, so the plate is angled slightly away from you. Then push it away with pressure from the fingers of your left hand, which are underneath, allowing the plate to slide onto the table.

If plates were so hot that I could smell them, I spread them out before taking them into the dining room. They cooled off quite rapidly. Another trick was to place a cold plate at the bottom of the pile. This enabled me to handle the stack, and by the time I reached the bottom of the stack, the cold plate had been heated by the other plates.

SERVING DISHES: Over the years we became so used to holding heavy dishes that we could carry enormous weights, and our wrists could withstand all but the heaviest pressure exerted by people helping themselves.

TO HOLD A DISH

A single dish should be held in the left hand. To hold it correctly, place it on the palm of your left hand and spread your fingers and thumb out beneath it. Steady it with your right hand, pressing the ball of your thumb on the rim of the dish. When steadying a deep dish your forefinger will lie crooked beneath your thumb, and the rest of your fingers should rest comfortably round the side and beneath the dish.

Approach the person you are serving from the side. Put your left foot forward, because you are serving from the left-hand side. Your foot should be as far under the table as is convenient and comfortable. It should be a step apart from your right foot to help you balance. Just as a boxer always has his feet apart to keep himself steady, so must you.

Lean forward by bending from the waist and slightly bending your left knee, so your body is relaxed. Bend your left elbow to bring the dish within reach of the person you are serving. If you hold the dish directly above your left foot, this will help you support the weight of the dish. Sometimes I would slide my right hand under a dish and hold the dish in my right hand while moving from one person to another. That split second made all the difference; in that time I could wriggle and stretch my fingers so that my left hand was less stiff when I took hold of the dish again.

You must stand relaxed and hold the dish as near to the plate as possible. It should be close enough that the person can help himself or herself and food cannot fall on the table. It mustn't be so high that it comes under the person's chin. When a footman first starts, he is so tense that he holds the dish near the ear of the person he's serving instead of near the plate. We used to watch new footmen like mad; they were so keyed up that after serving two or three people their arms began to ache, and there was a danger that they might drop the dish.

To serve two dishes at once, you must be very careful. It was a long time before new footmen were allowed to do so. Hold one dish in your left hand and the other in your right. If there is a choice between two dishes, such as a lemon mousse and a chocolate mousse, show the person you are serving both of them together. The left-hand dish should come a little in front of the right-hand dish, above your left foot, and the right-hand dish should be a fraction higher than the left-hand dish. The one that is chosen remains at serving level, and the other is held out of the way against your chest. Never hold it high or wide.

If there is no choice—you are simply serving two dishes, for instance broccoli and potatoes—offer the dish held in your left hand first. After the person has helped himself or herself, hold it to your chest. To offer the dish held in your right hand, bring your right hand level with the shoulder of the person you are serving. Then lower the dish to a convenient height for serving and turn out your wrist to bring it to the plate. This position puts considerable pressure on your wrist and can be painful if the person takes time looking for a tidbit.

Although I don't recommend it within your home, there is one trick that can hurry a person along. I've seen it happen on more than one occasion, and I must confess I have tried it. I was offering a heavy, hot dish that was burning my hand, and the person I was serving wouldn't take any notice of me. So I just caught the tip of his ear with the second hot dish—see him jump! And as we weren't allowed to speak, I couldn't apologize.

Put a serving dish down as you would a plate, using your fingers underneath it to gently push it away so it slides onto the table. And pick it up as you would a plate by slipping the fingers of your left hand underneath it and pulling it gently towards your hand until you can slide it onto your open palm. If you are not experienced at waiting, pick up the dish from the side with your right hand and place it firmly on top of your left hand.

A dish that is too hot to handle is picked up as follows. Hold a soft white napkin in your left hand, which should be close to—almost touching—the side of the dish. Then, holding a second napkin in your right hand, grasp the right-hand side of the dish and place the dish on the napkin on the upturned palm of your left hand. When carrying a hot dish around the table you can support it with the bare thumb of your right hand—we would always discard the right-hand napkin before moving with the dish. You may think it will be too hot for your thumb, but your thumb presses only against the edge of the dish to steady it, and the edge cools very quickly.

If I was offering a selection of vegetables on a flat dish, I held the dish on my palm and turned my wrist, and perhaps used my right hand to turn the dish by pushing the edge, so that the different vegetables faced the person I was serving. A flat dish was much easier to serve from than one with a handle. Since the handle was held in one hand, turning the dish placed a considerable strain on the wrist, particularly if the vegetables were at the wrong end. In a dish of this kind the heavier vegetables should be nearest to the handle and the lighter vegetables on the far side, and the handle should be grasped near the dish.

Meat and vegetables should always be served before sauce or gravy. The vegetable most recently come in season should be served first; for instance, early asparagus would be served before another vegetable. Potatoes are always offered last.

HOLDING A SALVER: I recently saw a butler on television handing letters to his master with his thumb over the rim of the salver. He was no more butler than a fly in the eye! I hold a salver on the palm of my hand, the same way I hold a dish. I crook my thumb round the back foot; if the salver has four feet, I crook my thumb round the foot nearest to it. The only time your thumb should ever appear on a salver is when you need to secure something on top of it, such as a sauceboat. And in that case your thumb would be hidden under the bowl of the sauceboat, steadying the base.

HOLDING A TRAY: A coffee tray usually has handles. I hold the tray with two hands and crook my thumbs over each of the handles, keeping my fingers underneath the tray as a precaution, in case a handle comes off.

HELPING YOURSELF

It made all the difference in the world to us if the people we were serving helped themselves correctly. The number of people who didn't was quite surprising! They would drop the serving spoon back into the dish without giving it a thought. And if I was holding two dishes, I hadn't a free hand to put things back in their proper order.

Serving utensils are placed for the convenience of the person being served, and they should be replaced in the same position. The spoon and fork should be together on the left-hand side of the dish, with the spoon to the right of the fork. After helping yourself to pâté or cheese, replace the knife so that the handle faces towards you. When taking gravy or sauce from a sauceboat, replace the ladle over the lip, not to the side, to keep the sauceboat balanced.

Before the war we served six courses every night—soup, fish, a main course, a sweet (such as a mousse) and a savory (such as mushrooms on toast), as well as fruit, which we called dessert and never thought of as an actual course. At a dinner party we might serve seven courses and dessert. The extra courses were an hors d'oeuvre and an entrée dish that was usually game. There was a handwritten menu in French in front of each person. People didn't necessarily eat every course; frequently a gentleman would say no to the sweet when we offered it to him and yes to the savory, whereas with ladies it was the other way round.

On party nights going in to dinner was a procession. There were place cards round the table, and each gentleman knew which lady he was supposed to escort into the dining room. After the butler announced dinner, we footmen stood quite motionless behind the chairs, then helped the guests push their chairs in when they sat down.

SERVING WINE AND LIQUEURS

SERVING FROM A WINE BOTTLE: Whenever I served from a bottle in the old days, I wrapped a white damask napkin round it to cover the label. The corners of the napkin crossed under the neck. If I needed to stand the bottle up on the table, I pinned the two corners together.

It is no longer considered necessary to hide the label, and it is much more sensible to hold a bottle without a napkin, as you can get a stronger grip. In fact, you might hold the bottle at the back, behind the label, so that if someone asks what wine you are serving, you can hold the label up for the person to see.

I grasp a single bottle firmly in my right hand so that my wrist is above the bottle. My forefinger presses against the shoulder; my thumb is about an inch below the shoulder at a slight angle, opposite my second finger, which is pressed against the body of the bottle on the other side. I feel holding a bottle this way gives me more control than grasping it round the neck.

I approach the person I am serving from the side. And as drink is served from the right, I put my right foot forward a step in front of my left. I position my right foot under the table at the point where the glasses are.

Then I bend my elbow and pour wine into the glass until it is three-quarters full, which is as full as any wineglass should be. I always give the bottle a little flick at this stage, in case there's a drop left on the lip which could run down the side of the bottle or fall onto the table.

SERVING TWO WINES: When I'm serving two different wines, I hold the bottle I think will be less popular in my left hand. It is much harder to pour from this hand when serving from the right. To pour with my right hand, I simply bend my wrist forward towards the glass. Pouring with the left hand means bending the wrist backwards to reach the glass, which makes for greater strain.

I generally knew which wine a guest would choose, as I had usually served him or her before, and a good butler always remembers. So if I was sure the person I was about to serve would prefer the bottle in my left hand, I would step back behind the chair and come forward again on my left foot.

I never altered my grip on the bottles when I carried them round the table. I held both of them upright so that the lip of each bottle came level with my rib cage. When I was pouring from one bottle, I held the second bottle against my lower chest, which meant it came above the shoulder of the person I was serving.

SERVING FROM A DECANTER: Red wine was always served from a decanter. A decanter should be held firmly round the neck, just under the lip, so that it is ready to pour. If I was serving from both a decanter and a bottle, I would always hold the decanter in my right hand and the bottle in my left, because a decanter is more awkwardly shaped for pouring.

SERVING LIQUEURS: After dinner the ladies left the gentlemen to their port and brandy and retired to the drawing room, where we served them liqueurs. We didn't want to disturb the gentlemen by popping back into the dining room for liqueurs, and we also wanted to save our feet, so we learned to carry a number of bottles at once. The most that could be managed was four. I would carry three in my left hand. With the palm upwards, I would take the neck of one between my little finger and third finger, one between my third finger and middle finger, and one between my middle finger and forefinger. In my right hand I carried the fourth bottle. If I knew beforehand who wanted what, I placed the correct bottle in my right hand and arranged the bottles in my left hand in the proper order. After I served the most important guest from the right-hand bottle, I would hold it between the thumb and forefinger of my left hand and take one of the left-hand bottles in its place. It is not advisable to serve liqueurs this way unless you have practiced.

People say you should rest after a meal. I rarely had time to do that when I was working. The pantry staff (the footmen and the butler) were always having to jump up in the middle of their meals. There were the last-minute things to do before a meal was served in the dining room. A footman, for instance, would have to draw the water or beer for lunch, put ice in the dining room and take in the cream and cheese and biscuits. If guests were expected, everything had to be ready in the dining room before they arrived, so we could receive them at the front door. I was very lucky if I had more than ten minutes for my meal, and if I was called away from the table by a bell, I never went back. But in spite of this I have never had indigestion in my life.

WASHING UP

The secret of caring for cutlery, china and glass is the washing up. Everything must be washed, rinsed, properly dried and carefully put away. It is important to know how to do these things correctly.

As far as I am concerned, if you have to rinse your plates before loading them into a machine, you might just as well wash them by hand. Of course, dishwashing machines are tremendously labor-saving; when we were in service, we spent hours washing pieces that nowadays could go straight into a machine. But the usefulness of these machines definitely has limitations. For safety's sake, delicate or valuable pieces of china or glass must be washed by hand. All silver must be hand washed, as it may be scratched if it is done in a machine, no matter how good the machine is. Proper hand washing of silver also is a necessary step in polishing it.

Barbara and I wash up between courses, so that by the time we've finished eating, most of our work is done. If you are not adept at washing up, this may be impractical, particularly if you are entertaining a large group. You risk breakage if you attempt to wash up hurriedly in order to rejoin your guests. But if this is the case it is absolutely necessary to scrape any remaining food off the plates and stack them tidily after each course. When you leave one plate here and another somewhere else and the knives and forks spread about, you're filling up space uselessly, and it takes no longer to put one plate on top of the other. You should stack by the sink. If you don't have room on your draining board, put a table by it.

RINSING

Except for nongreasy items such as glasses, everything should be rinsed before washing. Rinsing halves your work, leaves the washing water cleaner and ensures that everything will be properly cleansed. Rinse china and cutlery soon after use to prevent food from setting. Then you can come back hours later, after your guests have left, and start washing up. Never leave it for the next morning, as it will be ten times as much work.

We always rinse our cutlery by pouring a jug of water over it. Our draining board slopes towards the sink, so the water will drain into the sink and not splash onto the floor. If your board is not built at an angle towards the sink, it probably has grooves etched in it which will trap water and channel it into the sink. If your draining board is flat and without grooves, you would be well advised to have it rebuilt at a steeper angle towards the sink, so that the water can drain quickly.

CUTLERY: To rinse cutlery my way, lay spoons and forks on their sides in neat rows on the draining board and pour three-quarters of a jug of hot water (about a quart) over them. Lay the knives flat and pour tepid water over them.

PLATES: Rinse plates one by one so they don't become chipped. Lay them face down at the side of the sink ready for washing, each overlapping the next by half.

If you do not have time to rinse each item separately, fill the sink with water and add a few drops of detergent. Rinse knife blades and lay the knives on the draining board; you should never soak knife handles. Stack your plates in the sink with spoons and forks laid neatly on top. I keep my knives out of the way – having rinsed the blades first – on the left draining board. If you leave handfuls of spoons and forks soaking at the bottom of the sink, they will become scratched. Stack your silver properly if you like to see it clean, rather than looking like a bunch of old iron.

You can leave soapy water in your pans and serving dishes to prevent food from congealing, but it's better to wash cooking utensils as soon as you've finished using them. Cleaning them as you go along will give you more work space and will leave you less washing up to do later.

EQUIPMENT FOR WASHING UP

You need one or two dishpans, detergent, a soft bristle brush or nailbrush, a fine cotton string dishcloth, disposable dishcloths such as Handi Wipes, soft lint-free cloths or Irish linen tea towels (we have always got two if not three in use, because when one becomes wet it must be changed for a dry one). You also need steel wool pads for scouring heavy-duty pots and pans, and nylon pads for nonstick kitchenware. People with sensitive hands should protect them by wearing rubber gloves. I just plunge my hands in water, but then I am always careful to use hand cream afterwards. You should also have a draining rack and perhaps paper towels for mopping up–I wouldn't use them for drying.

I prefer to wash up in a dishpan, because most sink stoppers are not watertight and a dishpan holds water better. If you are washing up in a dishpan, any water that slops over the side can run down the drain, whereas if you are washing up in a sink full of water and it splashes over, you and the kitchen floor are both going to get wet. And finally, it's quicker to empty water out of a dishpan than to drain the sink. Plastic dishpans are better than enameled metal ones because they don't scratch. In the old days we used small wooden ones that were made for us by a cooper.

Until after the war, our "detergent" was a soft soap that we whipped into a lather with whisks like those used for cream, but three times as long. Nowadays a mild detergent does an excellent job. To make detergent lather faster, sprinkle powder or squirt liquid into your sink before adding water. If your water is hard, add a drop of ammonia–enough to cover the bottom of the bottle cap–for a softening effect.

A nailbrush is good for scrubbing a breadboard or forks; the bristles winkle out any food particles that have been allowed to dry between the tines. As a rule, if you wash forks straightaway, this won't happen. The bristles should be soft but stiff enough to pass between the tines. Our brushes, which were slightly larger than nailbrushes, had soft natural bristles that didn't scratch the silver.

WASHING

Some people are fussy and some people are not, but in my opinion washing up well means inspecting each individual piece and seeing that it's perfectly clean. It is the duty of whoever is drying to return anything that has not been properly washed. And if you're washing alone, it would be quite wrong to ignore a plate that is even slightly smeared. You can examine each item more minutely if you wash and dry them separately; it is as quick a way as any, and pieces are less likely to become chipped or scratched if they do not rub against one another.

Wash glasses (the least greasy items) first, then spoons, forks, knives, plates and serving dishes. If your pots and pans are not already out of the way, clean them last.

Finish washing up one set of items before going on to the next, as things are easier to rinse while they are still wet and easier to dry while they are still warm. I wash, rinse and dry my glasses before going on to my silver, and my cutlery is ready for storing before I start on my plates and serving dishes. Because you rinsed the food from the items before you began washing them, your washing-up water should be nearly as clear at the finish as it was at the start. You can wash all your glasses in the same dishpan of water, change your water and wash all your cutlery, change your water again and wash all your plates. I wash glasses and knives in tepid water, and the rest of my washing up is done in hot water, as hot as my hands can stand it.

The pantry staff were responsible for seeing that plates arrived at the table clean, because we were the ones who actually put them in front of the lord and lady. When the kitchen people washed plates, they might be a little careless, but when the pantry people washed them, they shone. I used to watch the plates like mad. If I ever came across a dirty plate, I whisked it away at once and changed it, and I always checked them thoroughly before a party to make sure we wouldn't arrive in the dining room with seven instead of eight.

FINAL RINSING

If washing up isn't thoroughly rinsed, it will dry smeary and dull. Everything but glass and bone-handled knives should be rinsed in very hot water, which evaporates quickly so the items will dry much faster.

The way Barbara and I rinse is to pour three-quarters of a jug of water over each set of items, so none of our washing up is left sitting in rinsing water surrounded by its own suds. Instead of pouring a jug of water over your items you can fill a dishpan with clear water and briefly immerse each one.

Either pour warm water over glasses, letting it spill over the rim of each glass, or immerse each one in water and then stand it upright on the draining board. After rinsing a glass, leave a little warm water at the bottom to keep it from becoming cold. Warm glass is much easier to dry than cold.

DRYING

Anything that has been washed in hot water and rinsed and stacked will already be half dry. Finish drying with a smooth Irish linen tea towel or lint-free cloth. Either one should be soft, as a rough cloth may leave scratches. You should hold the towel or cloth in both hands when handling the items to avoid leaving fingermarks.

TO DRY AND POLISH PLATES: Never pick up a plate with your bare hand when you come to dry it; take hold of it with a cloth so as to avoid fingermarks. Then rub it briskly back and front.

If your plates have been properly washed and put away, all you need do is polish them when you take them out of the cupboard before a party. You must, of course, make sure that you have the right number and that they are in good order and not cracked. When I was a footman, there'd be at least a couple of us at work if there were a tremendous number of plates to polish. But I can polish a hundred plates in twenty minutes, because after all I've been doing it for fifty years.

HOW STANLEY AGER POLISHES A PLATE

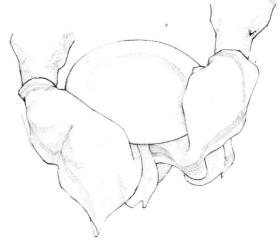

To bring up a greater shine, polish each plate after you dry it. To polish the rim, take hold of the plate with a tea towel. Hold it in both hands, the front facing you. Your fingers should be spread out on the back of the plate, and both thumbs should be holding the tea towel against the front of the rim. Now turn the plate by bringing your right hand up to meet your left, then your left hand down to meet your right. The plate will turn anticlockwise.

Now polish the front and back. Holding the plate steady in your right hand, rub the front and back briskly in a circular motion with the tea towel held in your left hand. When you have made a few quick turns, hold the plate up to the light to see if there are any marks. There shouldn't be; the plate will be clean and shiny.

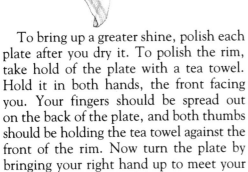

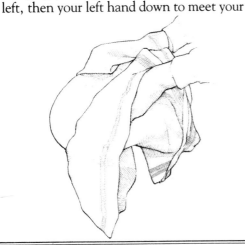

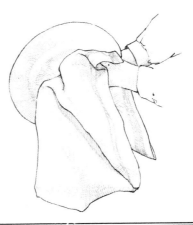

TO DRY AND POLISH GLASSES: We always polished our glasses when we took them out of the cupboard, paying special attention to the feet of stemmed glasses, which attract dust. Some people would wash them instead of polishing, but this is necessary only if the glasses have been kept in storage for some time.

If you have properly washed and dried your glasses, you can usually get away with polishing them once as you are laying the table. Once you have positioned a glass correctly on the table, pick it up with a clean Irish linen tea towel and polish it. After this point it must not be touched by human hands, because even if your hands are cool, they will mark a highly polished glass. When you replace the glass, make sure the tea towel protects it from contact with your forefinger and thumb.

TO POLISH A GLASS

Holding the tea towel in both hands, pick up the glass. Tip the warm water out of the bowl. Insert part of the cloth into the bowl and turn the glass upside down so it rests on your right hand (thumb in bowl, fingers loosely holding the outside of the cloth-covered bowl). The upturned bottom, also covered by the cloth, is supported gently by the left hand. Now turn the glass clockwise with your right hand, and help it turn in this direction with your left hand. (This will in fact mean your left hand moves anticlockwise.) The glass will rotate. Never hold the glass tightly. If you hold one end of a wine glass rigid while drying it, you will wring its neck. If you put too much pressure on the top of a tumbler while turning the bottom to dry it, a sharp triangle of glass will probably come away from the rim.

Even when you know the glass is quite dry, carry on turning it two or three times to bring up a brilliant shine. This is known as polishing a glass.

REMOVING STAINS

TO CLEAN A DECANTER: The butler's traditional method of removing sediment from a decanter is with water containing salt and shot from a cartridge. This is not as extravagant as it sounds, because you can save the shot and use it again: simply strain it from the decanter and keep it in an eggcup or similar small receptacle.

Fill the decanter with half a pint of warm water and add a couple of teaspoons of salt and the shot from a cartridge. Grasp the neck of the decanter with your right hand and support the base with your left hand. Swirl the mixture round and round inside the decanter until any sediment has come away from the sides and base. Pour out the mixture into a sieve, saving the shot. Then wash the inside of the decanter with a little detergent and warm water. Again, holding the dcanter firmly at the neck, with your left hand supporting the base, swish the detergent mixture round the decanter. Then empty it out with a jolly good shake.

Thoroughly rinse the decanter two or three times. For the last rinse fill it one-third full of warm water and empty it. Then take hold of a tea towel with both hands, grasp the decanter in your left hand and briskly dry the outside of the decanter with your right hand.

You obviously cannot reach into a decanter to dry it. The best way to dry the inside is to turn the decanter upside down and shake it. A decanter can be heavy and slippery, however, and there is some danger that it will go crashing to the floor if you don't hold it properly.

To hold a decanter securely, wrap a tea towel around the body and funnel, or neck. Place your hands on it, palms down, as follows: let your forefingers intersect behind the base of the funnel and your other fingers cross in front, resting on the shoulder (where the body widens). Use your thumbs to support the base. If your thumbs do not reach the base, let them rest comfortably but firmly beneath your forefingers. Now turn the decanter upside down and shake it two or three times.

TO CLEAN TEAPOTS: A silver teapot needs a thorough scouring at least once a year to remove the tannin or tea stain. Put in two teaspoons of washing soda and fill the teapot three-quarters full with boiling water. Allow it to stand for an hour. Then wrap a dishcloth round the handle or bowl of a wooden spoon and take it round inside the pot. Pour out the mixture–it will come out the color of tea. Look inside the pot and repeat the exercise if it is still stained.

Rinse it thoroughly three or four times with boiling water and then immerse the pot in detergent and water. Wipe the outside with the soapy dishcloth and then rinse the teapot two or three times under running water. Make sure there is no soap left on the outside or the inside–if you can smell soap on the inside of the pot, it needs to be rinsed again. Dry with a clean tea towel. Then clean the outside of the pot with silver polish.

In the ordinary way I never wash my china teapot with soap. I simply remove the tea leaves or tea bags and rinse it under running water; the last rinse is always cold.

To remove tannin, clean the inside of the teapot once a year if your water is soft or twice a year if it is hard. I use a British product called Ariel to remove the tannin, although I believe that Gain is just as good. For a medium-sized teapot, put in a half teaspoon of detergent and then half fill the pot with boiling water. Let it stand for about five minutes; then wrap a dishcloth round the handle of a wooden spoon and wipe the inside of the pot with it. The tannin should come off onto the cloth.

You should rinse out the pot three or four times with boiling water, then give it a last rinse with cold water. The water from the final rinse must be absolutely clean. After you empty out the water, smell the pot to make sure no trace of soap remains. The inside should be quite clean before you stand the pot upside down to drain.

TO CLEAN A COFFEE POT: Simply rinse silver coffee pots with boiling water–soap should never go near them. A china coffee pot can be washed in warm water with mild detergent when you are washing your coffee cups.

TO CLEAN CHINA CUPS: I see many tea and coffee cups with unattractive brown tea and coffee stains, but these stains are very simple to remove. All you need do is moisten your finger and dip it in some salt, then rub it over the stain. The discoloration will vanish almost immediately. Wash the cup afterwards.

Sometimes, the inside of a cup turns yellow because the china is crazed–that is, minute cracks have formed in the surface. In such cases there is nothing you can do.

TO CLEAN PANS: You can remove burned-on food from a heavy-duty pan by boiling a quart of water in the pan with a tablespoon of soda added. When you see the burned-on material loosening, empty the pan and rub it with a steel wool pad. Then rinse and dry.

The best way to remove a stain from an enamel pan is to boil raw rhubarb in the pan. When we have rhubarb, we check to see if one of our pans is discolored, and if one is, we clean it by using it for this purpose. Barbara stews half a pound of rhubarb in a medium-sized pan with half a cup of sugar and half a cup of water. The pan is cleaned by the acid in the rhubarb.

TO CLEAN A BREADBOARD: My breadboard is made of blond wood and is much softer than chopping boards that are used for meat and vegetables, which are generally made of teak. You shouldn't use a breadboard for anything but cutting bread, or the taste of other foods, such as onion, will linger and flavor the bread. These other substances can also leave unsightly stains on the board.

I have seen some truly disgusting breadboards. People forget to wash a breadboard, even though they have used it three hundred and sixty-five times during the year and it has absorbed grease from bread and fingermarks. Your breadboard should be scrubbed once a week. Dampen the board, then lightly sprinkle it with Vim, a scouring powder, and scrub it with a brush. An oval or oblong brush such as a nailbrush is easiest to grasp firmly when scrubbing. Then rinse the board under cold running water and stand it up to drain. Allow to air dry.

MAINTAINING WASHING-UP EQUIPMENT

SEA SPONGES: We used to wash dishes with sea sponges, which were cheap in those days. Nowadays they are expensive. Using sea sponges for washing up is perhaps extravagant, but they are excellent for this purpose or as bath sponges.

Sea sponges are easily cleaned. Put your sponge in warm water with a small measure of ammonia–two teaspoons of ammonia to one and one-half pints of water. Leave the sponge soaking in this mixture overnight, and it will be perfectly clean by morning. I don't like synthetic sponges, which can't be cleaned properly.

DISHCLOTHS: There's no need to wash disposable cloths such as Handi Wipes, as they don't last long enough to need special washing. Whenever they are being used, they are being washed with soap, which is all they need. Rinse them under cold water after you have finished washing up. (In fact, I do this with all my cloths.)

A cotton string dishcloth lasts longer than the disposable type and picks up more dirt. Sometimes I scrub mine the same way I do dusters and floorcloths. To do this, simply hold the dishcloth under the water and scrub with a household bar soap. To really bring dishcloths up white, rub bar soap on them and then boil them in an old pan, in a quart of water with a dessertspoon of soda added. The soda will clean them beautifully. Or you can boil them with two teaspoons of detergent to half a pan of water. But be careful the latter doesn't boil over.

SCRUBBING BRUSHES: These are cleaned by being constantly immersed in washing water. All the same, I rinse a brush after I've finished using it. Then I flick my brush two or three times to get rid of excess water.

TEA TOWELS: The secret of keeping tea towels clean is to wash them frequently. Most people just put them in the washing machine with the rest of their white things, but we boil ours separately in a large saucepan. We sprinkle detergent over them, cover them with water and let them boil for about five minutes.

Barbara likes to iron Irish linen tea towels after she has finished the rest of her ironing. It only takes a minute and is well worth it because if they are not ironed they become hard. She does the same with any soft drying cloth.

Old tea towels are very much softer than new ones. If the housekeeper gave us new tea towels, we moaned like anything and usually washed and ironed them before using them on glass or silver. Shops make tea towels stiff so they will look nice and presentable, but this makes them hard to the touch and less absorbent. Use a new Irish linen tea towel (sometimes called a glass cloth) only on china until after its first wash. Then it will be a very fine cloth indeed and ideal for drying glass or silver.

STORING TABLEWARE

I line all my drawers and shelves. Sticky-backed plastic shelf lining is excellent as it can easily be wiped clean. Take a damp sponge or cloth and run it over the lining a couple of times a year to keep it dust free and to flush out any insects that might have found their way into your cupboard.

CHINA

Specially good china such as Crown Derby or Royal Worcester needs special care. I place tissue paper or a doily on each plate and each saucer to protect it from the back of the next when I stack them in their separate piles. The back of a plate can be scratchy; it is never as smooth or as well glazed as the front. The lid of a fine china serving dish should be wrapped in tissue and stored upside down in its dish. Do the same with the lid of a good china teapot.

It is a good idea to hang all cups on small hooks above the shelf. It keeps them out of the way so they are less likely to be broken and frees useful shelf space.

For long-term storage, cover your china with a piece of brown wrapping paper or stiff white paper. Tuck the edge of the paper under the china at the front of the shelf. Then fold the paper back over your china. When you close the cupboard door, there will be a slight draft, so hold the paper in position at the back by placing a roll of cloth or a saucer on top of it. Or you can lay the edge of the paper along the back of the shelf and hold it in position under a saucer at each end. Then tuck the paper under the china at the front. For additional protection hang a sheet of tissue paper from the top shelf so that it falls in front of the bottom shelves.

GLASS

Storing glasses in matched sets makes it easier to keep track of them. I can see exactly where a sherry glass is in my cupboard and I can take it out easily. But if claret glasses and tumblers were mixed in with my sherry glasses, I might catch one of them with my sleeve trying to find the sherry glass I wanted.

I never wrap glasses. Paper absorbs damp, and if glass is stored in a damp atmosphere over a period of time, it becomes cloudy. To my knowledge there is no household remedy for this. Also wrapping and unwrapping it would mean fussing, as well as extra polishing. Abide by the law of averages—the more you handle a glass, the more likely you are to break it.

I wouldn't dream of placing a glass upside down on my shelf. A glass stored this way will draw up moisture and become cloudy after a time. It will pick up the smell of the shelf, especially if the shelf is painted and not papered; this of course ruins the taste of wine or port.

Don't stand glasses so close together that they touch or they will clink as they expand and contract with changes in temperature.

It is always wise to throw away a cracked glass. One day it will let you down, particularly if the crack is in the thin stem of a wineglass.

I dislike seeing glasses stored on glass shelves, because they are apt to stick. The extra bit of force need to draw them apart could even result in wringing the neck of a wineglass.

To protect glasses from dust and save on shelf space, stack them in tiers. This is a safe, practical method for storing matching glasses, one I have used all my life. We usually made three tiers, but the number depends on the weight of your glasses and the height and width of your shelf. It is not advisable to store heavy modern glass in this manner.

HOW STANLEY AGER STORES GLASSES

Arrange a row of glasses a quarter of an inch apart. Lay a sheet of paper cut to the width of the row across the top of the row. Brown wrapping paper and thick white paper are both ideal because they are strong and porous. Lay the dull side of the brown paper on the glass; the shiny side should be face up.

When you lay out the second tier, it is important to center each glass between two of the glasses on the bottom row. Again, each glass on the second tier must be a quarter of an inch away from the next. The top glass should be finely balanced between the two underneath it, which share its weight. Build the third tier the same way. Each glass should be a quarter of an inch from the next and balanced between two glasses on the second tier.

Lay a sheet of tissue paper across the top tier to protect it from dust. As additional protection, hang a piece of tissue paper from the top shelf so that it falls in front of the shelves below it.

SILVER

Silver should be kept in a dry place at an even temperature of approximately sixty-five degrees Fahrenheit. A soft lined drawer, box or tray, with wedges separating the pieces, is best for keeping everyday silver. Store all knives, spoons and forks on their sides. Never put one on top of the other because the bottom piece must take all the weight, and silver can become scratched if it is stacked. Your silver must be thoroughly washed before you put it away.

If silver is going to be stored for over a month, you must polish it first. For long-term storage it is best to line your silver cupboard or drawer with shelf paper and wrap the silver to protect it from dust and keep it from tarnishing. It is particularly important to wrap silver if you are storing it in drawers or shelves that are lined with baize. Baize is susceptible to damp, and if it becomes damp it can smell abominably and your silver will pick up the smell.

WRAPPING: Never wrap silver in newspaper, because the print will mark it. You can store silver tableware in a soft fabric bag or wrap it in old damask napkins. Personally, I prefer to wrap all my silver—tableware and large pieces—in tissue paper. It must be strong white nonacid tissue paper, not the yellowish acid tissue paper, which tears easily. Never stint on tissue paper—use two or three sheets. If you use a single sheet, the corners will have slipped or the silver will have come through before you know where you are.

There is a special way of wrapping tableware. To wrap it correctly, place a piece on its side on tissue paper, a few inches from the edge. Fold the tissue over the first piece before laying a second piece beside it; this way each piece is protected by a layer of tissue. At the finish you will have a long parcel. Tuck the ends under for neatness.

Make separate parcels of identical knives, identical spoons and identical forks. You must never mix different cutlery together; each parcel must contain items of exactly the same shape and size, so that you can recognize what is inside by touch, without opening the wrapping. When I go over to the castle now, I can just go to the silver chest and pick out any packet they happen to need. I know exactly what kind of piece is in each one by the feel of it.

Silver can hold its shine for years if properly wrapped. At the outbreak of the war I wrapped Colonel Trotter's silver in tissue paper and put it away in the silver chests. It wasn't taken out until I returned from the army five years later. We unwrapped it in the morning and were able to use it for lunch the same day. This is the beauty of knowing how to wrap silver properly.

OTHER GRACES

The people that I worked for were very correct and extremely well mannered. Both the servants and the people we served took great care and pride in doing things the right way. In my view this very special way of doing things is the key to graceful living.

ROYAL OCCASIONS

It was easy as winking to entertain royalty, because all of the work had been done beforehand. If it is an official visit, they invite themselves through the Lord Lieutenant, who is the Queen's representative for his county. He is given instructions from Buckingham Palace, and the police are notified. If it is an unofficial visit and you are a personal friend, then the procedure is quite different.

I remember when Frank, one of my footmen, began working for Princess Marina, the Queen's aunt. He was startled one day to see an unfamiliar lady walking across the hall. He went off to find the butler. "I saw a lady just now, and I think it was the Queen," he said. And the butler replied, "That's all right, she often comes, she's here for tea. There's no reason to worry about her." He had known in advance that the Queen would be there, but it was an informal visit and no one had wanted any fuss or bother.

Because it was to be an official visit, I knew by January that the Queen Mother was coming for lunch at the Mount in May. I knew that she was going to arrive at noon and leave at half past three so she could see the garden, have lunch and look round the castle.

Gradually everything was pieced together. Her Ladyship told me who was being invited, and we decided on the silver and what service to use. About a month later she said, "Well, we'd better start thinking about the menu." Both of us began making suggestions, and we reached our final decision about six weeks before the day. Because the lunch was in early summer, we decided to start with a cold course–salmon mousse–followed by a light main course. Then we would have a strawberry compote and finish with dessert and cheese. As strawberries would be out of season when the Queen Mother came, I ordered them specially from my friends in Penzance. I also told them I wanted new carrots–not French ones, the English ones.

The cardinal rule is never to tell your staff that you're entertaining royalty until just before the event. The gardener was warned to tidy up the garden, and my staff knew they were preparing the castle for May 4, but they weren't informed why until the night before. I knew well in advance because I was Her Ladyship's right-hand man. Unless she was a very trusted retainer the cook wouldn't know as soon as the butler, because cooks are not nearly so discreet as butlers.

It didn't matter whether the Queen Mother, or an old family friend, or even a disagreeable person was being entertained; as far as we were concerned, a guest was a guest, and that meant we had to do things properly. The blotting paper was fresh, the brass cleaned, glasses cleaned, carpets cleaned and so on. Of course we paid a little more attention when royalty came; extra provisions were ordered, and I made absolutely sure that every room the visitor might pass by was clean in case she wanted to look inside. When the Princess Royal stayed, she asked to see the boiler room by the front door because she passed it regularly and had often marveled at how hot our water was. In the ordinary way a boiler room is not on top of anybody's list of places to clean and is easily forgotten when you're busy. But having had experience with these people, I saw that it was tidy. Another place they visited was the tram, a small underground railway truck that brought stores up to the castle. The second boiler room was nearby, and before you knew where you were, they were looking at that.

Whenever royalty came into the room, and any time I was approached, I bowed with a nod of the head. We were always ready to open the door for royalty and we always knew their whereabouts exactly.

Usually they were gracious enough to meet the staff before they left. When the Queen Mother came, Her Ladyship asked me to have the staff in the dining room by half past two. The Queen Mother thanked me for looking after her, and I introduced each member of staff.

When royalty comes, the police look after security. A CID plainclothes detective came to see me about a month before the Queen Mother arrived. He greeted me with, "We've had some inquiries–what staff have you got?" I asked him to come into my office and I shut both doors. He asked me exactly who my staff were and personal details about them. It was my responsibility to be answerable for the staff we had, but he wasn't only vetting them, he was also vetting me. Her Ladyship and I had already discussed the staff. If we had been unsure of anyone, that person would not have been at the castle by the time the Queen Mother came. We wouldn't have employed any new staff until afterwards.

When the Princess Royal came to stay on an official visit, she had to have top security. This meant there were police in the castle and patrolling the island. But they could never be sure which entrance she would use–the public one on the west side or the east entrance, which was private. Well, the Penzance policeman who was supposed to follow her at a discreet distance would come into the pantry, which overlooks the east door, whenever he had a chance. He passed his time drinking coffee or beer and smoking himself to death. I came in one day and said, "Look here, Johnny, the Princess Royal has gone out the other door."

He replied, "You're not kidding me with that one!"

"She's gone out the west door," I insisted.

"No, she goes out this door," he said.

"Johnny, look, for heaven's sake. She's gone, you'll be in trouble." But he wouldn't believe me.

"I tell you what. Come to the dining room and look out of the window, and you can see for yourself," I suggested finally. So we went into the dining room and looked out. "There's the Princess on the causeway!" I said. "And you know how fast she walks, she rushes like a train."

Johnny went beating down after her, but he was a fat policeman and not quick on his feet. He was too late. The chief constable was there and had of course noticed his absence. Poor old Johnny didn't come back to the Mount, and there was a new policeman at teatime.

BEING A GUEST

You should reply to an invitation at once. Arrive at a party promptly, especially if the host is a particular friend; it is only the first few people who ever see all the trouble that has been taken. After that the room is chockablock and nobody notices anything. If the invitation says from seven till eight, it means exactly that, and I think everyone should be gone by ten minutes past eight. And if you are invited to arrive at eight, for dinner at half past, I would arrive a little after eight.

If you arrive punctually, you can leave more easily. You must stay a minimum of twenty minutes at a drink party or reception—a quarter of an hour is just a bit too short. The earliest you can leave a dinner party is three-quarters of an hour after you have finished eating, which gives everyone time to have coffee and digest their meal. Don't ever stay so long that you become an unwelcome guest. Be particularly careful not to do this at a drink party, when the few people still left may be waiting for you to leave because they have been asked out to dinner by the host. As a general rule leave a dinner party before midnight, especially if it is being held midweek.

Anyone who turns up without having answered their invitation is asking for trouble and should expect a cool reception. This happened to a young lady at a ball at Buckingham Palace. An equerry said to her, "Oh, I'm surprised to see you here." "I'm so sorry not to have answered the invitation," she dithered. "Don't worry, my dear," he replied. "It was our fault for inviting you."

It is common courtesy to thank your hosts before you leave, even if you are at a large reception and they are hard to find. Ideally you should write a thank-you letter the following day for a dinner party or for a weekend stay. You can write within the next ten days, but leaving it any later is rude. Nowadays people telephone their thanks; this should be done within a couple of days.

DEALING WITH SERVANTS

I believe the two most daunting concerns guests have when they are first asked to stay in a house with staff are how to behave towards servants and what to do about tipping.

As far as tipping goes, you should tip the person who looks after you. A maid will look after a lady, and a butler or footman will take care of a gentleman. She or he will unpack your bag and repack it when you leave, wake you in the morning and look after your clothes. And the best way to tip this person is to place the money in his or her hand with a word of thanks when you are called the last morning of your stay. The amount is of course up to you, but I think that two pounds (approximately five dollars) for each day is a reasonable sum. If you have not been properly looked after, you should pack your own bag and keep your money.

When Mrs. Vanderbilt came to stay at a house where I was footman, everyone from the butler to the hallboy, and from the housekeeper to the scullery maid, received a tip. The lower orders were given a pound and the amount increased according to the person's status in the house. The night before she left, each of us was given the tip in an envelope with a request for a receipt. The receipts were collected and sent up with her breakfast tray next morning.

Butlers have to be emotionless and therefore we seem cold and intimidating to guests who aren't used to us. But once a guest comes to know one of us a lot of the strangeness disappears. When dealing with servants, just be your own natural self. Don't pretend to be aristocracy if you are not. The real people don't regard servants as servants; they regard them as human beings—same as themselves, near enough.

Servants belong to a particular house—at the castle I seemed like part of the furniture. When I left to go work elsewhere, guests who knew me at the previous house recognized me straightaway, and it was all very friendly. Royalty are good about such things. Four days before war was declared, Princess Alice said to me, "Well, goodbye. Goodness knows if we shall ever meet again."

And I didn't see her until thirty-one years later, when we met at a wedding reception. I always rode a bike when she stayed with the Trotters in Scotland, and this was how she remembered me. "I can't remember your name," she said, "but you're the butler on the bicycle."

The people who don't get on with servants are the ones who walk past them with their noses up in the air. But it is also wrong to chat to servants for hours on end, because for one thing they are busy and haven't got the time.

As a rule, most guests who were staying for a weekend arrived in time for tea. They would say "Good evening" to us as they came into the house. We wouldn't say it first because servants are not meant to speak unless spoken to, so it was really up to the guests to open the conversation. When passing the time of day with servants, you might remark on the weather: "This is really like summer!" When you are waiting for your host to appear, and the butler comes in to straighten the cushions, you can admire the view from the drawing room window. You could also talk about how the garden has changed since you last stayed. Another opening gambit is the birds on the estate: "Do the peacocks keep you awake at night?" One guest told me he'd been advised to lay down Taylor's 1908 port and asked what I thought. I replied that it was the most lovely port, but he was thirty years too late. "It's going to cost the earth now, and it's going to be quite chancy, because it's getting on, " I told him.

We didn't have much trouble with the real people, except for one or two who were known to be difficult. Be we had to deal with quite a few brash young men during the London season. They were mostly living on the cheap, on the lookout for an heiress.

Our comeback was slight if the offender had only been invited for a dinner party. Then we'd just turn his kid gloves inside out after he gave us his coat, before slipping them back into his pocket. It's an awful job to right those kid gloves when they are inside out–and it's certainly not easy for a young man to do when going out with a young lady in a hurry.

If one of these horrible young men had come for the weekend, we might weaken a couple of stitches in the instep of his shoe by half cutting them with a razor blade, so that a couple of weeks later the sole of his shoe would hang off. We never cut the stitches all the way through, just enough to come apart sometime after he had left us. The other trick was to half cut a few stitches in the seat of his trousers, so that when he sat down a couple of weeks later the back seam would come apart.

A maid will call a lady in the morning, and a butler or footman will call a gentleman. It is quite enough to say "Good morning" when the servant enters the room, because then he or she knows you are awake and can say "Good morning" back to you. I never needed to turn on the lights because I knew the layout of the room. I'd come in and draw back the curtains, then I'd put the tea tray by the bed.

Servants are there to help you, so never be afraid to ask if you have a query. But don't ask your host's servants about protocol. You can discuss this only with your father's butler if he is an old family retainer.

You may feel intimidated when a butler asks you for your case keys in order to unpack for you. You think, "My God, I've only thrown my things in." That doesn't really matter. If you're a nice person or a young person, the butler will straighten you up.

What you must not do is unpack by tipping your case upside down on the floor. A guest did this to me once, and when I came in to draw the curtains I walked over everything. "This is a frightful mess," I told him. He apologized: "I'm sorry about the mess, I was in a hurry to unpack." "I can unpack quicker than that," I replied. "You don't need to drop your things on the floor and leave them. Your drawers are empty and your wardrobe is over there. I'm not having anything more to do with you." And I didn't. I never picked up any of his things; he had to pick them all up himself. His wardrobe was disgraceful, but when he asked me to press his trousers, I said, "No. I'm not going to press your trousers, because all those creases in them are unnecessary."

One of the real secrets of being a good guest is to keep the place tidy. It's not your house, it's not your own room. What you would do at home you should not necessarily do in someone else's house. The staff will gladly do what they have to do for you–unpack and pack for you, call you in the morning, brush your clothes, clean your shoes–but they won't spend twenty minutes picking your clothes up off the floor.

EVERYDAY GRACES

TO OPEN AND CLOSE A DOOR QUIETLY

On party nights two matched footmen stood ready to open the doors leading to the reception rooms. They were both six feet tall, wore identical liveries and had similar features. So that the guests would have no trouble acknowledging them, whoever stood on the left was called John and the other was addressed as James, regardless of their real names.

You never heard a footman actually close a door, it was done so quietly and discreetly. I open and close a door the same way today. The trick is to release the door handle only once. Most people open a door, let go of the handle, walk through the doorway, take hold of the handle again and shut the door. But after I have opened a door, I keep the handle turned until I have passed through the doorway. Then, without releasing the catch, I take hold of the handle in my other hand. I hold it in the same position until I have gently closed the door and the catch is ready to click into place.

TO STAND STILL FOR LONG PERIODS OF TIME

This is one of the things that all footmen learnt, as we often had to do it when on duty. I am glad I have this knowledge; I have found it useful on all sorts of occasions, even when I haven't been working.

The secret is simple; you must be relaxed. You should stand with your feet eight inches apart, hold your normal posture and keep your head firmly upright–not poked forward or leant back.

We stood with our hands behind us, so that if we needed to flex our fingers we could do so without anyone seeing us. I once worked under a butler called Pack, who loved to play practical jokes. He came behind me when I was standing on duty one night and popped a hot potato into my hands. I didn't know what the devil to do with it, so I put it in my tailcoat pocket. But then of course it started burning the back of my thigh, which was even more sensitive than my hands! I think Pack was the most eccentric butler that I ever worked under.

TO HELP SOMEONE ON WITH A COAT

Hold a coat at the midpoint of each shoulder. Make sure the coat is positioned so that the person can easily slip his or her arms into the sleeves.

You must make sure that the collar of the garment underneath is hidden by the collar of the coat. A man's overcoat is usually slit at the back. As you lift the coat onto his shoulders with your right hand, you can reach inside the coat and pull down his jacket with your left hand to settle the jacket collar inside the overcoat collar. Alternatively, after you have lifted the coat onto the person's shoulders, lift it again immediately to settle it over the clothes underneath. This is what I do when I help a lady on with a coat.

TO IRON A NEWSPAPER

When the newspapers arrived in the morning, we clipped the top and bottom of the center pages with special newspaper clips, rather like large paper clips, so that none of the pages would fall out of place. Because they were full-size papers, not tabloid size, we folded them in three horizontally, from the bottom to the middle to the top. Then we laid them out in neat rows on the drawing room table, arranging them so only the names of the papers and the headlines were visible.

We had to keep them looking fresh and crisp, so we ironed them as soon as they became crumpled, which might mean three or four times during the day. Some people screwed the paper up in a ball and then threw it down in disgust if they read something they disagreed with, whereas others managed to crumple a paper simply by handling it. (We always knew who these people were, but then we knew everybody's bad habits.) We ironed the papers on the pantry table. It took only a couple of minutes to press each one.

To iron a newspaper, you need a warm iron (hand-hot is usually hot enough). Press the back and front pages with it, starting at the top of the page and working downwards. There's no need to iron the rest of the paper; the heat and pressure of the iron will flatten the intervening pages. Nowadays you must clean your iron afterwards, in case the soleplate is marked by the newsprint.

Only the better newspapers, such as the *Times* and the *Financial Times*, were read in the drawing room. I certainly wouldn't bother to iron the cheaper ones–they are not worth the trouble, and the print is very likely to come off.

TO ROLL AN UMBRELLA

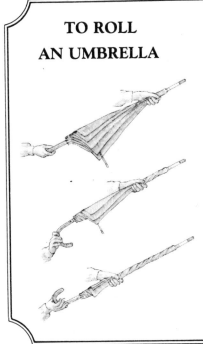

To begin, grasp the handle in your right hand and hold the umbrella in front of you. Make sure the folds of the umbrella are lying smoothly, one over the other. I arrange it so that as many as possible fall to the left side of the stick.

The next step is to curl your left hand around the tip of the umbrella and catch the ribs together. I like holding the ribs fairly tightly. Then turn the handle clockwise with your right hand, and at the same time–without relaxing your grip–bring your left hand toward the handle of the umbrella. This pulls the ribs tightly together and flattens the folds, so that you finish with a slim-looking umbrella. Then all you need do is fasten it to hold the ribs in place.

HOW STANLEY AGER TIES A BOW TIE

Most men wear a black bow tie on formal occasions with a dinner jacket. Bow ties are made of black satin, crepe satin or velvet. They are made in different neck sizes, and it is important to buy the right size. A clip-on bow tie saves you making the bow but is not nearly as attractive as the old-fashioned bow tie that you tie yourself.

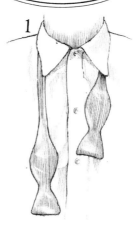

1. Put the tie around your collar. The tie should lie flat, and one end should be three to four inches longer than the other.

2. Cross the longer end over the shorter end.

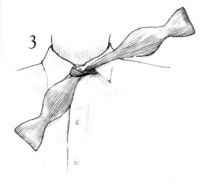

3. Make a knot by passing the longer end behind the shorter end.

4. Let the longer end hang over the shorter end.

5. Pull the tie tight around your neck. Make a fold in the shorter end at the point where it flares to its bow width. Bring the folded portion up and hold it so that the fold points toward the longer end and the narrowest part is at the center.

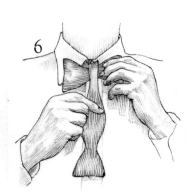  

6. Bring the longer end down over it. The shorter end is now in position to form one half of the bow. Hold it in place.

7. Fold the longer end at the point where it flares to its bow width. Bring the folded longer end up behind the folded shorter end and pass it between the shorter end and the knot (arrow).

8. The fold must emerge behind the single side of the shorter end. You will now have a loose knot.

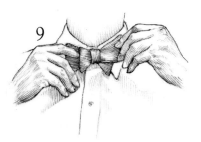 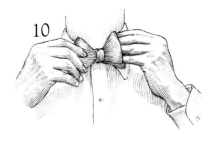

9. The front and the back bow are each composed of a single and a double end. To tighten the bow, first take hold of both double ends and pull them tight.

10. Then center the bow by gently pulling the two single ends. You will feel the knot loosen to some extent, but overall it will have tightened. You may have to repeat this exercise two or three times before it is tight enough.

A white tie is tied exactly the same way as a black bow tie. Up until the last war gentlemen wore white tie and tails to dinner and the ladies wore long dresses, but white ties are rarely worn nowadays.

TO PUSH IN A CHAIR CORRECTLY

Despite your good intentions you can put someone on the floor if you don't know how to do this properly!

Whatever you do, you must not tilt the chair. As the person is bending his or her knees to sit down, take hold of the back of the chair with both hands and place your foot underneath the chair. Then ease the chair forward by bending your knee, and at the same time gently push the back of the chair with your hands.

TO TELL A WHITE LIE

We had to be discreet and reticent and protect our employers from unnecessary intrusions. On occasion this called for a white lie. The most common one was required when a member of the family gave instructions that he or she didn't wish to be disturbed and then someone came to call. In this case we would simply say the person was not at home.

This often happened when someone came to call on Lady Dunsany in London. She would leave a card lying on the hall table that said "Not At Home." This warned us to tell any visitor that she was out, even if we knew she was in. Sometimes a caller would insist, "But I saw her go in." This made no difference. "You may have seen her go in, but she's not at home," I'd say politely but firmly. Then the visitor knew she was unavailable and would leave a card for me to give Her Ladyship. And she returned the compliment of their call by sending back her card. One of the footmen would have the chauffeur for the afternoon and be driven round London delivering all Her Ladyship's calling cards.

TO LIGHT AND SMOKE A CIGAR

There is an art to lighting and smoking a cigar. Smoking without haste is the secret and the key to enjoying it. Most men seem to understand this; they smoke only one large cigar a day, last thing after dinner, when they have time to sit back and relax. A cigar that is smoked slowly will be cool to draw on. If you puff away like a train, you will burn it quickly and ruin the taste, and it will have a red glow on the end as though it is in flames. You should be able to smoke a cigar so slowly that you have about an inch of ash hanging off the end. A decent cigar will last anywhere from half to three-quarters of an hour.

The first thing to do is take off the advertising band round the bottom of the cigar–just tear it off. If you are smoking a cheap cigar, you don't want anyone to know, and if you are smoking an expensive one, you shouldn't show off.

An expensive cigar is handmade, and one end, called the cigar cap, is sealed to prevent the cigar from drying out in storage. In order to draw smoke through a cigar, you must cut off the cap or pierce the end. You can pierce a cigar with a cigar cutter or with the end of a matchstick. Personally, I think you should cut off the cap *and* pierce it to allow for a greater passage of air, which will make the cigar easier to draw.

I would use a match to light a good cigar. I certainly wouldn't use a lighter because it will leave the taste of lighter fluid in the cigar afterwards, which will completely spoil the fragrance. In the old days our table lighters burned methylated spirits, which made for a taste-free flame that was perfect for lighting a cigar. One of these lighters was passed round on a silver salver after the men had been handed their cigars.

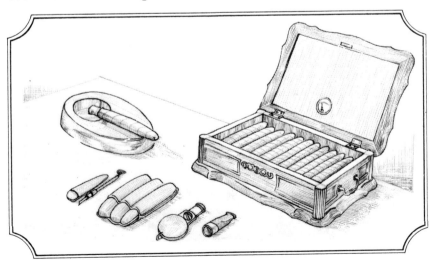

You should never light a cigar by putting the flame directly on the tip. Instead, hold a lighted match close to it–almost touching–and draw the flame to it by gently puffing on the end. It is quite wrong to light a cigar quickly; it should take at least three or four seconds. You will need to puff the cigar two or three times to keep it alight.

Smoking, like lighting, should be done gently and without haste.

TO LIGHT AND SMOKE A PIPE

A good many of the gentlemen I worked for smoked pipes, and it was part of my job as valet to see that they were always filled. I used to fill six pipes for the second lord in the morning and leave them in his pipe rack. Then at lunchtime I refilled the pipes he had smoked and put them behind the unused ones in the rack.

I don't recommend a cheap pipe. A badly made pipe will become very hot and make you cough as you draw on it. A good pipe smokes coolly and has a completely unseamed body–with an attractive grain if it is briar.

A bowl should be tight enough so that the tobacco won't burn quickly, but you shouldn't pack your pipe too tightly; it should be loose enough to burn without effort. I would light a pipe, like a cigar, with a match and not a lighter, to avoid the taste of lighter fluid. Don't puff hard at a pipe, but let the smoke come to you, the same way you would smoke a cigar.

Tap the ash out of the bowl after you have finished, but don't tap your pipe on something hard or you could easily crack it. A lot of people very sensibly use the heel of their palm.

A man should always carry cotton pipe cleaners to remove the nicotine and saliva from the pipestem. I found that using pipe cleaners that had been dipped in vodka, a tasteless solvent that evaporates quickly, was an excellent–albeit expensive–way to clean the stem. You should also have a pipe scraper (this usually looks like a penknife) to scrape the excess tar from the bowl. How often you clean a pipe depends on how much you smoke, but you should clean it thoroughly at least once a day, either last thing at night or before using it in the morning.

ROMANTIC PICNIC FOR TWO

For true elegance you must plan well ahead. People on a romantic picnic aren't likely to have much appetite, so it is the quality rather than the quantity of food that counts.

FOOD

I would suggest soup; whether you take it hot or cold depends on whether the day is cool or warm. There is nothing romantic about a thick broth, but a rather exotic soup such as lobster bisque, which tickles up the palate, is perfect for the occasion. A clear jellied consommé is very refreshing. I also recommend turtle soup. It can be served hot or cold, and when it is served cold it is absolutely delicious. Keep the soup in a thermos.

Follow the soup with pâté. Some pâtés are rough and others are smooth; I would take one of each, and of two different flavors. Pâté can be served in one piece with a long roll of French bread, which can be broken apart rather than sliced, or made into sandwiches between thin slices of brown bread that have been cut in four. Wrap the French bread and the pâté separately, and put the pâté in a plastic container. Do the same with pâté sandwiches. You can also serve pâté between thin slices of toast. Seal the toast in aluminum foil or plastic wrap and spread it with the pâté when you arrive at the picnic.

Pâté should be served with salad, which travels well when wisely chosen and packed correctly. Keep it simple.

I would wash a small lettuce and put it in a plastic bag before placing it in a plastic container. Then I might wash and slice a cucumber and a couple of green peppers and wrap them to keep them succulent. I would add some radishes for a dash of color—wash them first and trim both ends before wrapping. Put the salad ingredients together in a plastic container and put it in a cool place to stay fresh—a cooler is ideal. I would prepare a delicious salad dressing and put it in the cooler with the salad. Dress the salad immediately before you eat it.

I would end the picnic with fresh fruit. I suggest strawberries and cream, or apples and oranges. You must wash fruit beforehand. If you are offering apples, polish them so that they are left shining and keep them in a container so that they don't become dusty. You would of course pack strawberries in a container.

DRINK

Choose a favorite white wine. Make a special effort to take one of the best–an ordinary bottle of cheap wine is not especially romantic!

Half a bottle of wine or champagne should be enough for two. If you take a bottle you should finish it, and if a man produces a whole bottle his companion may think he is trying to make her drunk. If a lady is making a picnic for a man and he is driving, she should take this into consideration. Half a bottle allows one person a single glass and the other person two glasses. It's a question of judgment: if both of you normally drink two glasses of wine, you might take two half bottles and open the second one if need be.

It is easier to offer brandy or a liqueur after coffee than an aperitif before the meal, which entails ice and yet more bottles to carry. But if you know that the person you are treating has a particular liking for, say, whiskey and water, then you must take it.

COFFEE: I would take a thermos of black coffee rather than tea, especially if I had decided to end the meal with a fine brandy. Tea was never served after a meal in the large houses as it wasn't considered an appropriate drink before a liqueur. A pint of cream should be enough for both your coffee and your strawberries. I would also bring a container holding granulated coffee sugar.

PICNIC EQUIPMENT

I would keep my wine, pâté, salad, butter and cream in a cooler and carry everything else in a hamper or basket, which always looks attractive.

GLASSES: As this is a special occasion, you might like to pack wineglasses or champagne glasses, and brandy rummers or small tumblers for liqueurs. When packing stemware, wrap tissue inside and round the bowl, round the stem and round the foot. Don't stint on tissue; stemware needs a great deal of cushioning. Wrap small tumblers in tissue paper and fit one inside the other. Place them in a corner at the front of the hamper, where less weight will bear on them.

PLATES: Again, for a special occasion I would take china plates. You could buy two different patterned plates–a special dinner plate for each of you to commemorate the outing. If you are using china dinner plates, each of you must have a china soup plate or bowl and a china dessert plate for your strawberries or fruit. Pack a small wooden bowl for the salad.

Pack the plates first. Put a doily inside each soup bowl and between the plates, and wrap them in parcels of tissue paper before putting them in your hamper.

KNIVES, SPOONS AND FORKS: It is tempting to take silver, but silver scratches easily, and I wouldn't want to see it lying on the ground or have the worry that a piece might be lost. Sadly, I think one must take stainless steel. If you are using soup plates or eating jellied consommé, you need two soupspoons. Each person should have a knife and fork for the salad and pâté, as well as a dessertspoon and fork for the strawberries and cream. Apples and oranges require a small knife. Remember to take a spoon and fork for serving salad, teaspoons for sugar and coffee, a knife for each of your pâtés and a butter knife.

COFFEE CUPS AND SAUCERS: Wrap china coffee cups in tissue. Put doilies between the saucers before wrapping them in tissue.

ODDS AND ENDS: Pack a corkscrew, salt and pepper and a large garbage bag for cleaning up.

TABLECLOTHS AND NAPKINS: You must each have a linen napkin, and you should take a linen tablecloth on which to lay the food. I wouldn't advise taking a white tablecloth; it won't stay fresh for long, and white things require more laundering when they are stained. Pack the tablecloth and napkins last so that they don't become crumpled.

Lastly, take a thick rug to sit on, with a raincoat to put underneath if it is not waterproof.

INDEX

Stanley Ager entered service at the age of fourteen. He was butler at St. Michael's Mount for nearly thirty of his fifty-three years in service. Barbara and Stanley Ager currently live in Marazion, Cornwall.

Fiona St. Aubyn is an author who divides her time between New York and London. A granddaughter of the late Lord St. Levan and the Dowager Lady St. Levan, she has known Stanley Ager all her life.

St. Michael's Mount,
Cornwall